7/98

PHILIPPINES

Lily Rose R. Tope

MARSHALL CAVENDISH
New York • London • Sydney

Reference Edition published 1996 by
Marshall Cavendish Corporation
99 White Plains Road
Tarrytown
New York 10591

© Times Editions Pte Ltd 1994, 1991

Originated and designed by
Times Books International, an imprint of
Times Editions Pte Ltd

Printed in Singapore

Library of Congress Cataloging-in-Publication Data:
Tope, Lily Rose, 1955–
     Philippines / Lily Rose Tope.—Reference ed.
        p. cm.—(Cultures Of The World)
     Includes bibliographical references and index.
     Summary: An illustrated overview of the history,
geography, and culture of the Philippines and the people
who inhabit these tropical islands.
     ISBN 1-85435-403-5
     1. Philippines—Juvenile literature   [1.
     Philippines.]
I. Title. II. Series.
DS655T66 1991
959.9—dc20   91–15855
                          CIP
                          AC

INTRODUCTION

HISTORICAL TRIVIA has it that when the United States Congress was debating the American annexation of the Philippines, one representative asked another representative beside him what the Philippines was. The second representative paused to think and said that it must be the country of the biblical Philippians. On another occasion, an American boy of eight asked a Filipino exchange student whether or not Filipinos lived in trees.

This book is written for people who have an interest in learning more about this fascinating country. It depicts the Philippines as a tropical land of colorful diversity and complexity, and a nation with a fascinating mixture of races and traditions that contribute to the Filipino identity. This book, part of the *Cultures of the World* series, will also look at how the Filipinos see themselves and will acquaint you with the Filipino's unique culture.

CONTENTS

A Filipina, all spruced up, at a town fiesta.

CONTENTS

Zamboanga in Mindanao has been called the "City of Flowers." Here, at a local market, a boy sells the item that has made the city famous.

5

GEOGRAPHY

THE REPUBLIC OF THE PHILIPPINES is an archipelago of 7,107 islands splayed like a necklace that lies between latitudes 21°N and 5°N in the Western Pacific. Spread over a total land area of 115,830 square miles, it reaches northward toward Taiwan, while the southernmost tip almost touches Borneo. To the west is the South China Sea and mainland Asia, while to the east lies the Pacific Ocean. Slightly bigger than Great Britain, the Philippines has a coastline twice that of the United States.

The physical terrain of the Philippines is varied. Mountain ranges run through the entire island chain, contrasting sharply with the rich green lower slopes and coastal plains suited to agriculture. Early travelers saw the islands as gems and called the archipelago the "Pearl of the Orient." Fewer than a third of the islands in the archipelago are inhabited, and the largest 11 account for 95% of the total land area.

Opposite: **Mountain ranges in Ifugao Province, Northern Luzon, overlook impressive rice terraces carved out of the slopes of mountains.**

Left: **Pangasinan's famous "Hundred Islands" is located off the northwestern coast of Luzon. Rich in marine life, this area has the second largest collection of coral specimens in the world.**

Manila Bay along Roxas
Boulevard in Manila pro-
vides excellent protec-
ted anchorage. It has one
of the city's most beau-
tiful panoramas.

LUZON, THE VISAYAS, AND MINDANAO

The Philippines is roughly divided into three main areas: Luzon, the
Visayas, and Mindanao. Luzon, the largest island, is the most populated.
Metro Manila, home to about 10 million Filipinos, lies on the western
side. Due to its strategic river and sea location, it is the most logical seat
of commerce and government.

Luzon has Manila Bay, one of the world's best harbors, as well as the
largest area of level farmlands. It also has the highest industrial concentration.
South of Luzon is an island network collectively called the Visayas. Its most
important islands are Leyte, Negros, Samar, Panay, and Cebu. The city of
Cebu is the area's business and industrial center and is second only to
Manila in importance.

Further south is the country's second largest island, Mindanao, and the country's richest in terms of natural resources. Communities of Moslem Filipinos ("pili-PEEN-os") and other indigenous groups who resisted colonization have flourished here, hewing the island's culture closer to that of traditional Southeast Asia than to Westernized Manila.

In fact, despite the present-day dominance of Christian settlers, Mindanao remains culturally separate and neglected. Rulers in Manila have time and again been reminded of the possibility, albeit remote, of needing their passports to land in Mindanao.

MAYON VOLCANO

The queen of Philippine volcanoes, Mount Mayon (from the Bicol word "magayon," meaning beautiful) is located in southeastern Luzon. It stands at 8,000 feet, majestically exhibiting its perfect cone shape, undeformed by 33 eruptions in the last 150 years. The first eruption was in 1616, followed by a second one in July 20, 1766, which lasted six days. The most destructive was on February 1, 1814, when towns were buried in mudflow and ash. The belfry of the ruined Cagsaua church stands as a ghostly reminder of Mayon's wrath. The mountain has been quiet since 1984. The Bicolanos can only hope that they never again incur the ire of the capricious goddess and that she remains generous to them during their lifetime.

Taal Lake and Volcano at dawn, from Tagaytay Ridge. Situated on an island in the center of Taal Lake (which itself is the crater of an extinct volcano), Taal is the lowest active volcano in the world and the most destructive in Philippine history.

LAND OF FIRE AND HEAVING EARTH

The Philippines' geological birth was accompanied by volcanic processes and adjustments in the oceanic plates, causing islands to rise and fall and resulting in the creation of mountains and trenches.

Not all geological occurrences were dramatic though. Coral, which thrives in the warm Philippine waters, accumulated to form island foundations. Later, during the Ice Age, land bridges connected the Philippine Archipelago to other islands and to mainland Asia. This explains the similarities in flora and fauna varieties in the Philippines and

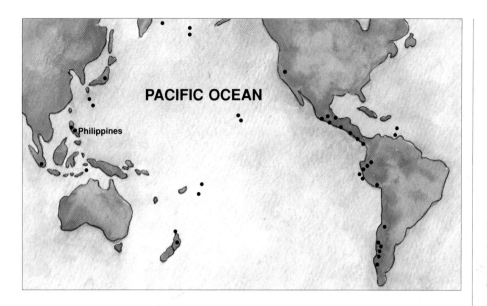

PACIFIC OCEAN

Philippines

The Philippines is located in an earthquake belt, commonly known as the Pacific "Ring of Fire." Dots on the map mark the major volcanoes in the area.

in Celebes, Moluccas, Borneo, and even Taiwan.

The Philippines is a land of contradictions. It is blessed with abundant natural resources, yet what nature has given, it has also taken away; a heritage Filipinos did not choose but must learn to live with.

The Philippines lies in the active portion of a zone of earth fractures around the Pacific Ocean called the Circum Pacific Seismic Belt or more simply, the earthquake belt. The country experiences one large magnitude tectonic earthquake (magnitude: 7.75 and above) every 10 years, seven earthquakes of major magnitude (magnitude: 7.0–7.4) every 10 years and five earthquakes of moderate magnitude (magnitude: 6.0–6.9) every year.

It is also a link in a chain of fire, a volcanic belt that rings the Pacific Ocean, and as such has about 21 active volcanoes distributed throughout the islands.

Although these volcanoes have caused extensive damage during eruptions, they have been responsible for the superior quality of soil around the volcanic areas in addition to being excellent sources of thermal energy. Among the major volcanoes are Mayon, Taal, Hibok-Hibok, and Kanlaon.

Above: **A quay destroyed by a typhoon in southwest Luzon.**

Opposite: **Orchids** (top) **and coconuts** (below) **grow in profusion all over the Philippines. The first coconut was believed to have been brought over from mainland Asia during the Neolithic period.**

CLIMATE

Like most of its Southeast Asian neighbors, the Philippines is generally warm (with an average temperature of 80°F) and has abundant rain. Seasons may be divided into hot, rainy, and cool. The months of March to June are very hot and dry; July to October are extremely wet months, while November to February are pleasantly cool and dry.

THE TYPHOON The typhoon is a strong tropical cyclone equivalent to the hurricane in North and Central America. It is characterized by the violent counter-clockwise spinning motion of the air that contrasts with a calm and clear core called the "eye." Typhoons, often accompanied by heavy rains, floods, and sometimes gigantic waves, occur during the months of the southwest monsoon (July to October). The intensity of a typhoon is known in the Philippines by its signals: signal 1 means winds of less than 39 mph; signal 2 means winds between 39 and 54 mph, and elementary and intermediate-level classes in school are suspended; signal

3 means winds of 55 mph and higher, in which case all classes are suspended and people are asked to stay indoors. In an average year, 21 typhoons enter the Philippines, resulting in 320 casualties, 686,000 people affected, and 7,200 homes and other buildings damaged or destroyed. Typhoons often travel in a slightly curved path from entry to exit, but they are also known to turn back not only once but several times or to mysteriously tarry.

FLORA

The Philippines has one of the world's richest varieties of plant life and is home to more than 12,000 species of plant. Of the flowering plants, the orchid family, is the largest with about 940 species, of which 790 are native. The Philippines is also covered with a lush plant growth both in the mangrove swamps by the sea and in the dense rainforests in the hinterlands that cover 15 million hectares, or nearly half the Philippines' total land area.

ABACA Known also as Manila hemp, abaca is a banana-like plant whose trunks are ripped lengthwise to be made into rope. In the 1800s, foreign seamen discovered its tensile strength and its ability to withstand the corrosiveness of the sea.

THE COCONUT Referred to in colloquial Filipino as the brain (as in the expression "use your coconut"), the coconut is called the tree of life because of its versatility. Every part, from the deepest root to the farthest frond can be used—for food, beverages, roofs and walls, jewelry, mattresses, paper, fuel, industrial products, and much more.

FAUNA

Called the "air's noblest flier" by aviator Charles Lindbergh, the Philippine Eagle, better known as the monkey-eating eagle, is one of the rarest birds in the world. Its height is over three feet and it has a wingspan nearly eight feet wide.

Land fauna is basically similar to that of the other islands in the region, particularly Borneo and Java. The ancient land bridges enabled the migration of species from the Southeast Asia. Traders and conquerors also brought several species into the islands, adding to the native stock. Bird species number about 800, and the marine fauna is considered the richest in Asia. Philippine reefs are famous for their size and the large variety of marine life they harbor.

Although a considerable number of animal varieties inhabit the islands, each species is represented by few individuals. True, this may be explained by the Philippines' archipelagic character, but also, humans are partly responsible. Consequently, animals known to exist only in the Philippines are now endangered. Tamaraw, the carabao's (water buffalo) smaller and wilder cousin, can be found only on the island of Mindoro. The monkey-eating eagle, the largest of all eagles, is the object of world-wide concern. Proud and sensitive, this eagle barely survived the reckless denuding of forests.

Other animals in danger of extinction are the mouse deer, Koch's pitta (a deep forest bird), the pelican, the nocturnal tarsier (the smallest primate), and the Sarus crane. Animals are also important as a means of livelihood. Of these, the most important to the Filipino peasant is the carabao. Patient and capable of backbreaking work, the carabao is considered the symbol of the Filipino's industriousness and perseverance.

METRO MANILA

For centuries, the old city of Manila was the nation's capital until someone, probably alarmed at Manila's decreasing space, ascending crime rate, and worsening reputation, decided to create a new capital in spacious, fresh, suburban Quezon City. For some reason, however, Quezon City was not popular. Manila's historical importance and fame cannot be ignored or forgotten. Today, the nation's capital is Manila once more. It is part of a metropolis called Metro Manila that has four cities (Manila, Quezon, Pasay, and Calookan), plus urbanized towns within a radius of approximately 50 miles. The most important are Makati (the nation's business center), Alabang, San Pedro, Novaliches, and Valenzuela—all industrial towns. By the end of the century, Metro Manila will span the width of Luzon to Infanta, Quezon, which faces the Pacific, making it one of the biggest city networks in Asia.

Called the Wall Street of the Philippines, Ayala Avenue is the financial hub of Manila. Here, vital business decisions and dollars are made.

Intramuros: Old and new buildings. On the right are the remains of the convent adjoining San Agustin Church, on the left a prizewinning new building built in the old style. Located within the confines of Intramuros, San Agustin dates back to the 17th century.

HISTORIC MANILA

Legend has it that the city was named after the *nilad* ("NEE-lud") plant floating on the Pasig River, thus its early name *Maynilad* ("My-NEE-lud"). Blessed with a fine harbor, Manila inevitably attracted explorers, traders, and settlers. When the conquistador Miguel Lopez de Legaspi found Manila, it was a thriving community. He built a wall around it, turned it into a fortress defended by moats and turreted walls 33 feet thick, and called it *Intramuros* (meaning "within the walls"). Except for a brief British interlude, the Spaniards were successful in keeping it insular and purely Spanish. However, the city outgrew its walls, so that by the time the Americans came, the walled city had simply become a district.

Manila has always been the seat of political power. Most colonial governors and all Philippine presidents resided in the Malacañang Palace by the Pasig River. Manila has also been the site of significant historical events such as the execution of José Rizal at Bagumbayan, the establishment of the Philippine republic in 1946, and the People Power phenomenon in 1986 that saw the overthrow of Ferdinand Marcos. Like the rest of the country, it has had its share of natural and historical catastrophes. In fact, during World War II, it was the world's most devastated city after Warsaw. Despite these events, it has survived and persisted. Like old wine, it has acquired more flavor with age.

MAJOR CITIES

CEBU The Queen City of the South, Cebu is the most important city in the Visayas and is the regional center of commercial and intellectual activity. It is the capital of the province of Cebu, whose not-so-arable soil is perfect for industrial development. In the nearby island of Mactan, Ferdinand Magellan was killed in battle by a local chieftain named Lapu-Lapu. A large wooden cross left by Magellan in 1521 now stands in a plaza in commemoration of the Spanish arrival.

DAVAO Davao is the largest city in Mindanao and the third largest in the Philippines. It is famous for its fruits—durian, lanzones, mangosteens, oranges, pomelos, and bananas. Its early inhabitants were the Manobos, a tribe famous for their exotic costumes and unusual musical instruments. A melting pot of sorts, Davao is now home to Ilocanos, Visayans, Tagalogs, Bicolanos, and Chinese Filipinos.

BAGUIO Called the summer capital of the Philippines, Baguio City rests on a 4,900-foot high plateau in the Cordillera Mountains. Its cool average temperature of 65°F and pine tree-lined roads make it a mecca for world-weary lowlanders.

HISTORY

THE SHORT, dark-skinned, curly-haired Negrito (Aeta) was once considered the Philippine Adam. Recent findings, however, show that they migrated to the islands from Southeast Asia more than 22,000 years ago.

After the disappearance of the land bridges, human migrations were by sea. One theory proposes the arrival of three groups, one of shorter, stockier people said to come from Indonesia and two of slimmer, slightly taller people of Malay stock. The latter drove the earlier inhabitants to the highlands and established communities along the sea and river areas. Before long, they evolved a lifestyle all their own, enhanced and enriched by influences from the Chinese, Arab, and Indian sailors and traders.

PRE-HISPANIC SOCIETY

Pre-Spanish peoples were grouped into kinship-based communities called *barangay* ("bar-RUNG-gai"), after the name of the seaworthy vessel on which they came. Early records show that an advanced civilization flourished, sustained by rice culture, fishing, weaving, mining, and trading. These people used a shell currency and a form of Indic writing inscribed on bamboo. They followed laws, were governed by a council of elders, and worshiped ancestors called *anitos* as well as the natural forces around them.

From the Chinese they acquired the use of porcelain, learned advanced methods of agriculture, and developed culinary sophistication. The Indians enriched the native language and script. The Arabs brought trade and Islam, the latter taking root in southern Mindanao.

Despite their seemingly cosmopolitan exposure, the pre-Spanish Filipinos had petty kinship rivalries and were divided. The Spaniards could not have chosen an easier people to colonize.

Opposite: **Legacy of the past—the ruins of Dingras Church in Ilocos Norte, built in 1598.**

Above: **Land bridges once connected the Archipelago with the rest of Southeast Asia and were used by migrating groups.**

19

Magellan's Cross, located at Plaza Santa Cruz, Cebu, commemorates the erection of a cross by Ferdinand Magellan when King Humabon and Queen Juana of Cebu, together with some 800 of their subjects, were baptized.

THE SPANISH CROSS AND SWORD FOR GOD AND GOLD

In search of another route to the Spice Islands, Ferdinand Magellan sailed for the unknown Indies and landed in the Philippines on March 16, 1521. Accompanied by priests, he started colonization by converting the chiefs and their families to Christianity. Five years later, a more determined expedition was launched, headed by Miguel López de Legaspi. Equipped with experiences in Mexico as a conquistador and an official, Legaspi succeeded in establishing a strong foothold in Luzon and the Visayas. He named the islands the Philippines in honor of King Philip II of Spain. He defeated the petty chieftains and rewarded those who participated in the conquests with vast tracts of land called *encomienda*, huge estates that were later worked by the natives and provided the Spaniards a comfortable life and prominent social status.

The Spanish Cross and Sword for God and Gold

An ardent nationalist who came from a humble background, Andres Bonifacio (1863–1897) advocated his own fiery brand of patriotism—armed revolution—in contrast with the non-violent reformist approach of his compatriot José Rizal.

Spain ruled the Philippines via Mexico. Huge bulky ships called *galleons* plied between Manila and Acapulco loaded with silk, porcelain, gold, and spices bound for Europe, bringing unmeasured prosperity to investors.

The Spaniards would not have been able to strengthen their position on the islands if not for the priests who tamed people's hearts. Convinced that they had to save the islands' pagan souls, friars embarked on a rigorous conversion campaign, Christianizing the majority of the lowlanders within a short time. They built churches, around which the town's social activities centered. They equaled and at times surpassed the civil government in influence and power. Separation of church and state did not happen in the Philippines for 300 years.

The Spaniards were hard taskmasters. They imposed forced labor and demanded unreasonable tributes from the natives, derogatorily called Indios. Even the clergy were known to be abusive.

Meek as they were, the Indios were often pushed to revolt but were easily quelled by the Spaniards' superior arms and "divide-and-rule" tactics. It was not until the 1800s that some form of sustained movement was born. The rise of the middle class saw sons of rich families acquire European education, and consequently, liberal ideas. Men of the Propaganda Movement worked for reforms and manifested strong anti-clerical leanings. Among them, José Rizal stood out. His arrest and execution fueled the fires of revolution that erupted in 1896. It was led by Andres Bonifacio, founder of a secret anti-Spanish organization called *Katipunan* (Brotherhood). On June 12, 1898, the first Philippine Republic was proclaimed.

JOSÉ RIZAL

Born on June 19, 1861, in Calamba, Laguna, of mixed (Spanish, Chinese, Filipino) parentage, José Rizal was a man of extraordinary talents. A medical doctor by training, he was also poet, philosopher, sculptor, scientist, folklorist, and spoke several languages. His mother, who was his first teacher and a great influence in his life, was falsely accused by the Spanish authorities and paraded publicly like a common criminal. This personal experience kindled in his young heart an anger against all forms of injustice. He proved that the pen is mightier than the sword by writing two novels, *Noli me Tangere* (*The Social Cancer*) and *El Filibusterismo* (*The Subversives*), that exposed the abuses of the Spanish government and the clergy. These novels galvanized the growing political awareness of the educated class, who later joined and led the revolution against Spain. For his activities, Rizal was executed on December 30, 1896, his death and his name becoming the battlecry in the struggle for independence.

THE AMERICAN ADVENTURE

The republic was short-lived. General Aguinaldo, head of the revolutionary forces, was exiled. In the meantime, the Spanish-American war broke out. In May 1898, Commodore George Dewey sailed into Manila Bay and destroyed the depleted Spanish naval fleet. The Filipinos aided the Americans, thinking they would be granted independence, but to their dismay the Americans landed as conquerors, not as allies. In December 1898, Spain ceded the Philippines to the United States for $20 million. Angered and frustrated, the Filipinos revolted against American rule and one of the bloodiest wars in history resulted.

A portrait group shot of General Aguinaldo and his fellow Filipino patriots in exile in Hong Kong in 1898.

The islands were finally pacified in 1902, the lure of economic opportunities and education for all too strong to resist. The United States saw its term in the Philippines as preparation for self-rule. It introduced American political institutions and processes, and opened the Philippine market to the West for economic self-sufficiency. Most importantly, classrooms were built to educate the Filipinos. Whereas the Spaniards refused to educate the natives "for their own good," the Americans made education available and compulsory.

By 1934, Manuel L. Quezon, who later became the first president of the Commonwealth, had been promised a Commonwealth by 1936 and independence by 1946. The transition would have been smooth had the Japanese not intervened.

THE THOMASITES

On August 21, 1901, a converted cattle ship called *Thomas* arrived in the Philippines carrying 540 American teachers who were assigned to the first public schools. They were not the first teachers. A smaller number had arrived two months earlier to supplement soldiers who chose to stay and teach after their tours of duty ended. However, the Thomasites, as they were eventually called, comprised the largest single group of teachers sent to educate and civilize their "little brown brothers." Of the 540 Thomasites, 27 died of tropical diseases or were killed by bandits during their first 20 months. Despite this, many stayed permanently and lent their time and talent to the cause of nation-building.

Box above: **A typical class during the American period. Through the American system of universal education, the English language spread rapidly throughout the country and remained.**

THE JAPANESE INVASION

On December 10, 1941, three days after the bombing of Pearl Harbor, the Japanese landed in the Philippines. They overran both Filipino and American forces, who made a last stand at Bataan and Corregidor. Forced to retreat, General Douglas McArthur pledged, "I shall return," a promise that Filipinos never forgot and that he kept in October 1944. Aided by local resistance fighters, the Americans reached the capital and engaged the Japanese in their fiercest battle. After the smoke had cleared, Manila was almost leveled to the ground. Sixty thousand lives were lost.

THE AFTERMATH

Immediately after the war, the Philippines was granted independence with Manuel Roxas at the helm. Extensive rehabilitation was needed, but due to an empty treasury, the Philippines sought the financial help of the

United States. Thus began the love-hate economic relationship between the Philippines and the United States, a factor that was to shape Philippine policy in the years to come. There were also rumblings of dissent from the peasants clamoring for agrarian justice. Defense Secretary and later President Ramón Magsaysay distinguished himself by quelling the unrest. His identification with the common people and his concern for their problems restored public confidence in the government.

Rusting cannons at Corregidor are some of the relics of war on this island fortress guarding the entrance to Manila Bay. They are a mute testament to the memories of Filipino and American forces who gave their lives defending it.

MARCOS AND THE MARTIAL LAW YEARS

In 1965, Ferdinand Marcos was elected president. In 1969, he became the first re-elected president. His term, however, was increasingly marred by economic setbacks, social unrest, and rampant corruption.

Corazon Aquino.

An astute statesman, Marcos initially rallied the people with his vow to make the Filipino great again. His initial achievements, however, were soon eroded by the excesses of his latter years in office. On September 21, 1972, in the midst of nationwide dissent, he declared martial law. He jailed his opponents, controlled the media, abolished Congress, forced the ratification of the 1973 Constitution, and established his New Society Movement. He and his wife, Imelda, isolated themselves and allegedly emptied the nation's coffers with their extravagant lifestyle.

CORAZON AQUINO AND PEOPLE POWER

On August 21, 1983, Benigno "Ninoy" Aquino, Marcos' exiled political arch-rival, returned to the Philippines and was shot dead on the airport tarmac. His death sparked widespread indignation that resulted in mass actions the likes of which no Filipino had seen before.

In January 1986, Marcos declared a snap election, challenged by Aquino's widow, Cory, who by then had become the anti-Marcos symbol. On February 22, Minister of Defense Juan Ponce Enrile and Vice Chief of Staff Fidel Ramos defected to Aquino. Millions of people trekked to the military camps to protect them from the Marcos forces. Three days later, Marcos left for an Hawaiian exile. The Philippine People Power revolution taught the world a lesson: that change can be achieved through peaceful means. Aquino's term in office ended in May, 1992. During her six years of presidency, democracy returned and there was some improvement in the economy. Despite these efforts, half of the population remained below the poverty line.

FIDEL RAMOS, THE CAN-DO PRESIDENT

With full support from Corazon Aquino, Fidel Ramos emerged victor in the peaceful presidential elections of May 1992. In a serious move to bring the country back to its feet, he focused on creating political stability by establishing peace with all his political rivals, including Imelda Marcos. The Communist Party of the Philippines, which had long created havoc in the country, was legalized and allowed to conduct legitimate political activities. Having established political stability, Ramos is aggressively focusing on economic recovery. Countries like Japan, the biggest donor of official development assistance amounting to $445 million in 1992–1993, Taiwan, and Singapore have pledged interests in various industries. Exports are to be developed as well, especially labor, since the unemployment rate runs to 50%. This excess could feed the desperate need for skilled labor in the Asian region, and is a strategy deemed to be one of the keys in reducing the level of poverty.

Fidel Ramos' inauguration on June 30, 1992.

GOVERNMENT

SINCE INDEPENDENCE, the Philippines has maintained a democratic government broken only by Marcos' autocratic rule. Since Marcos' abuse of power, the constitution was revised in 1987 to prevent prolonged tyranny from reoccuring. The Philippine government now has three independent branches: the executive, which administers the government; the legislative, which enacts laws; and the judicial, which enforces justice. Executive power is vested in a president, who is head of state and commander-in-chief of the defense forces. The president, who is assisted by a cabinet, serves no more than one six-year term and can approve or veto bills passed by Congress. Legislative power rests on a Congress that has two houses: the Senate (24 members) and the House of Representatives (up to 250 members), whose members are elected for six-year and three-year terms respectively. The judiciary is headed by a Supreme Court, consisting of a chief justice and several associate justices.

Opposite: **Baguio military academy cadets commemorate Independence Day with a splendid parade. Independence Day in the Philippines is celebrated on June 12.**

Left: **An imposing landmark, this old neoclassical Congress Building in Manila houses the Senate. Manila is the religious, social, cultural, and industrial hub of the country as well as its political center.**

LOCAL ADMINISTRATION

Government is basically centralized in the capital, Manila, but greater autonomy is now being given to the 15 local governments. At least two regions, the Cordillera and southern Mindanao, have been given full autonomy. The highest local unit is the province, which is run by a governor. Each province and city consists of several districts, each of which has a representative in Congress. Each district, in turn, is divided into municipalities headed by mayors, and these municipalities consist of *barangay* administered by the *barangay* captain. Cities are autonomous and run by mayors.

GRASSROOTS GOVERNANCE

The word *barangay* refers to the sea vessels in which the early settlers came, but it also connotes the kinship group to which every individual belonged. The modern *barangay* is no different except that in the urban areas, communities are not arranged by blood relations. The old *barangay* was headed by a *datu* ("DHAH-to"), the most prominent or wealthiest man in the village. He was assisted by a council of elders who saw to it that the ancient laws were followed. When the Spaniards came, the *barangay* chief became the tax collector and eventually the representative of the civil government on a local level. Today, the *barangay* captain does not collect taxes. With his councilmen, he settles petty quarrels between neighbors, screens newcomers to the *barangay*, maintains peace and order, and supervises social activities such as fiestas. Politicians court him for he can bring in the votes come election time.

Like the basic socio-political unit in the Philippines today, the *barangay* boat of old that traveled the waters of the Archipelago was made up of a well-defined community of people. Each *barangay* was capable of carrying from 60 to 90 persons, and each was led by a head called a *datu*.

Social activities, such as this re-enactment of an Ifugao rice harvest dance, are a part of life in a mountain *barangay* unit.

ECONOMY

THE YEARS 1993–1998 SHOULD BE EXCITING ones for the Philippines, as the new President Fidel Ramos has launched a no-nonsense economic improvement plan. In a country plagued by poverty, the hope of improvement lies in expanding investment and increasing traditional exports. All the prerequisities neccessary for these developments have to be in place: a reliable banking and communoications network, peace and security, financial aid, and a progressive work ethic. By developing an attractive atmosphere for investment, new jobs and industries will be created.

Blessed with natural resources, economic improvement is made easier. The Philippines is rich in minerals, especially copper, gold, iron, chromite, nickel, and coal. About two-thirds of the Philippines is covered with serviceable forests and 35% is agricultural land.

Opposite: **The Philippines is chiefly an agricultural country. Much of the farmland is devoted to rice, corn, sugarcane, and coconut plantations.**

Left: **The port of Manila, the country's most im-portant port, handles both domestic and international trade.**

AGRICULTURE, FORESTRY, AND FISHING

Philippine territorial waters have 2,400 known species of fish and mollusks. There are 120 fishing grounds, but most commercial fishing takes place primarily off Palawan, Negros, Mindanao, and Panay.

Agriculture is responsible for 45% of total employment and accounts for 23% of the Gross Domestic Product (GDP). Rice; fruits, and vegetables, especially sugarcane, coconut, bananas, and pineapples; coffee; rubber; abaca (Manila hemp); and tobacco are produced for domestic consumption and export. The Philippines is a major supplier of coconut oil and a contributer of sugar imports to the United States.

A diversification of agriculture is being encouraged to supplement the income of farmers through the co-cultivation of high-income earners like orchids, asparagus, and prawns. The success of this strategy was proven by Negros province in 1992. Fishing and aquaculture brought in $265 million in 1991, and are important industries that supply markets in Asia, particularly Japan.

The depletion of the forests that cover two-thirds of the country has reduced the supply of high quality timber and its products to Japan and the United States.

INDUSTRY

MANUFACTURING Comprising 25.5% of the GDP and earning $6,533 million in exports in 1992, the main earners in manufacturing are garments and electrical goods. Small- to medium-scale industries are encouraged in the production of garments, furniture, handicrafts, electronic equipment and parts, chemicals, glassware, and concrete products.

A large part of these manufactured goods is exported, and this is the main source of national income. The Philippines' main export partners, in order of importance, are the United States, Japan, and Germany. In the first half of 1992, 38% of Phillippines' exports were sold to the United States. As of 1992, the main import partner is Japan, which supplies transport equipment, vehicles, electronic machinery, and chemicals.

SHIPPING Following the United States' pullout of Subic Bay, various countries have been eyeing the Philippines' shipping facilities. Singapore's Keppel and Sembawang Groups have stated an interest in leasing Subic's ship-repair facilities.

CONSTRUCTION A boom in construction was evident in 1993 accompanying President Ramos' plan to revitalize the economy. New roads, hotels, and shopping malls have erupted all over Manila, Luzon, and Mindanao, and more projects are planned for the rest of the 1990s.

The stability of the region will not depend on the military presence of superpowers. It is economic cooperation and a common vision of what the region should be ... as well as what the condition of the world could be in terms of the reduction of weapons of mass destruction.

—Fidel V. Ramos

THE FILIPINO JEEPNEY

This mode of transport is affectionately remembered by tourists. A ride in a jeepney is a must if only to get a fleeting experience of the Filipino lifestyle. Their zest for fun, family values, religion, and their openess and simplicity all come together during the brief jeepney experience. The king of Philippine roads, the jeepney, is the descendant of the American World War II jeep, made longer, more colorful, and more Filipino. It can carry 17 passengers comfortably, but may be required to ferry double that number. Its flamboyant colors, decorations (buntings, curtains, etc.) and blaring stereo music are reminiscent of a town fiesta. A tiny chapel is enshrined on top of the windshield to ensure safe travel. Small stickers bearing jokes, some obscene, entertain passengers during long trips. Wherever the driver goes, his family goes with him: their names are lovingly etched on the dashboard. The mudguard contains his message to the world: God Bless You; *"Katas ng Saudi"* (literally, "Saudi juice") meaning "bought with Saudi money"; and *"Misis, mahalin si Mister,"* meaning "Wife, love your husband."

Burnham Park in Baguio provides a tranquil setting for those who want to get away from the bustle of life.

TOURISM

The Filipinos' innate warmth and hospitality to strangers are put to good use in the tourism industry. Blessed with a beautiful countryside and unique festivals, the Philippines has a lot to offer travelers. They may enjoy the comforts of luxurious hotels or rough it in a village hut. How can they go wrong in a place where everybody smiles? A major dollar-earner, the tourist industry caters to all kinds of pleasures—a day on a sun-drenched, wind-swept beach or a night in the honky-tonk.

For ardent shoppers, the Philippines has some of the finest ethnic handicrafts in the region. From Baguio and Paete, Laguna, come its best woodcarvings; from the Mountain Province the famous Lepanto cloth and handwoven baskets; from Mindanao brass and bronzeware; and from the Visayan chain of islands, musical instruments. The rich Philippine seas is reflected in its shellcrafts, which are always in demand. Philippine embroidery is a remarkable example of Filipino artistry that has made the Philippines a shopper's paradise.

MANPOWER

The Philippines has one of the highest literacy rates in the world, but ironically, it does not have jobs for the thousands of graduates produced every year. Due to the country's inability to sustain a steady economic growth rate, not enough jobs are generated to absorb the extra workers. Braving the uncertainties of life in a foreign country, many Filipino workers and professionals leave home and family to build a more stable future overseas.

Filipinos troop to the Middle East as engineers and skilled workers to man the region's industries. Filipino doctors and nurses serve its hospitals. While the Middle East has the highest concentration of overseas workers, other countries have their share as well. Filipino entertainers spice up the nightlife in Japan. Domestic helpers in Hong Kong, Singapore, and some European cities allow housewives to work or to pursue other interests. The Filipinos' relative proficiency in English makes them very marketable.

Above: **The Filipinos are a highly literate people. More than 80% of the population are able to read and write.**

WORK ETHIC

The Filipino is very cordial even at work, unlike Westerners who are often businesslike. Western business people often come bluntly to the point. Filipino business people generally like small talk and refreshments before business. In fact, business may sometimes become the postscript rather than the main agenda.

Filipinos put great value on their self-esteem or *amor propio* ("ah-MOR PRO-pio"), and are terribly upset when criticized in front of others. Therefore employees should be taken aside when pointing out mistakes and the discussion should end cheerfully by enquiring about their family. The Filipino will never disagree with anyone openly, and may tell a white lie rather than turn down someone openly.

Most offices resemble a big family or an urban village. The boss is the paterfamilias, strict and demanding but protective and congenial. Everybody knows everybody else and the coffee break, a Filipino must, is a time to catch up on the latest office romance or to plan the outing after work. Filipinos often small-talk while working. This is not negligence but a sign that one still remembers the existence of co-workers, no matter how urgent his or her task. Teasing the boss is not disrespectful but a means of personalizing professional relationships and establishing camaraderie with superiors. Though the described work ethic is very much a part of the Philippines' lifestyle, President Ramos is trying to increase productivity and efficiency to make the Philippines more competitive internationally.

Above: **Smooth interpersonal relationships are the Filipino way of life, whether at home or in the work- place.**

FILIPINOS

THE PEOPLE OF THE PHILIPPINES are usually categorized into three groups: the Christian lowlanders, the Moslems, and native animists. Although the terms suggest religious groupings, these are based on cultural rather than racial or religious differences.

About 90% of Filipinos are Christian lowlanders. Most are farmers and fishermen if they are in the rural areas; many are professionals and urban workers if they live in the cities. The largest group, the Tagalogs, live in central and southern Luzon, especially in the capital. The Visayan-speaking groups predominate in the central Philippines, while a hodgepodge of Luzon and Visayan migrants make up the Christian settlements in Mindanao.

Moslem Filipinos, sometimes called Moros, are found in southern Mindanao and the Sulu Archipelago. The Tausugs and the Samals live by the sea, while the Maguindanaos and Maranaos live inland.

The native animists inhabit the more inaccessible parts of the country. These are the hardy G-stringed men of the Cordilleras, the shy Aetas in their mountain lairs and seaside coves, the Mindanao hill tribes distinguished by their colorful costumes and rituals, and the gentle Mangyans of Mindoro. In 1971, a Stone Age community was discovered in the dense rainforests of Cotabato. The Tasadays, whose culture seems to have been preserved in time, have become the subject of much scholarly debate.

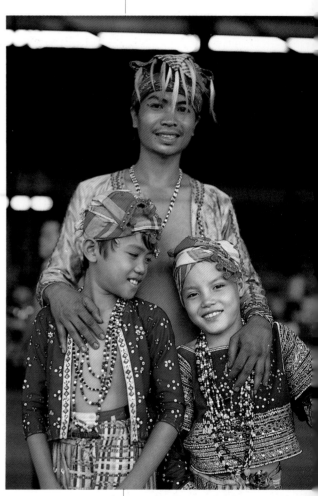

Opposite and above: **Filipinos are basically of Malay-Polynesian stock, with Chinese and Spanish ancestries.**

Below: **A *mestiza* around the turn of the century.**

Opposite top: **Dressed up in Barong Tagalog, a straight-cut shirt worn outside the trousers, Filipino men perform a dance at a social happening.**

Opposite bottom: **The Maria Clara dress is a lightweight blouse with embroidered sleeves and a striped-paneled skirt.**

MIGRANTS

Except for the ethnic tribes, there are few Filipinos who can claim to be racially pure. Somewhere in the past, the Filipino has acquired Chinese, European, or Indian genes. The Spaniards were free to intermarry with the Indios, although this was not encouraged among the upper classes. In the case of the Chinese merchants, it was convenient to have local wives who would help run the business, especially in dealing with local customers. (These merchants usually had families in China, but were not allowed to bring them to the Philippines. The same was probably true of the Indian traders.) The results of this racial intermixing were people called *mestizos* ("mis-TEE-sos") who were initially regarded with disdain or distrust. As they proved themselves capable individuals and as intermarriages became more common, the stigma slowly faded.

THE FILIPINO DRESS

Pre-Spanish-era men and women wore clothes according to the dictates of climate and modesty. Men wore a sleeveless jacket over loose trousers for greater air circulation. Women in the upper classes wore jackets with longer sleeves for modesty and long skirts that allowed them to walk gracefully. Many of the common women, however, were less concerned with modesty than with comfort. Some wore flimsy upper garments or none at all. Men and women often adorned their bodies with tattoos.

The Spaniards were scandalized by the women's near nudity and required them to wear long billowy skirts and blouses made of very fine fabric. A triangular scarf-like material crossed over the women's bosom, protecting them from prying male eyes. The dress is called the Maria Clara ("Mah-RIAH CLAH-rah"), after José Rizal's heroine.

Today, such dress is worn only on special occasions. The Filipina has gone through the European ballroom gown, the tassled shift of the roaring 20s, the padded shoulders of the 40s, the bellbottoms of the 60s, and the androgynous look of the 80s.

The men have the *barong tagalog* ("BAH-rong Taa-GAH-log") as traditional wear. Made of finely woven *piña* ("pin-NYAH") from the fibers of the pineapple plant or *jusi* ("JU-see") from banana tree fibers, the *barong* is worn on formal occasions. Men, too, have gone through the cumbersome three-piece suit of the 20s, the cuffed pants of the 40s, the leather jackets of the 60s, and the Wall Street attire of the 80s.

Metro Manila aides in their ubiquitous yellow uniforms at the Rizal Day celebration. Yellow uniforms were actually issued during the days of Imelda Marcos when she was the governor of Metro Manila. Later, it became the badge of support for the Cory Aquino government.

THE POLITICS OF FASHION

Clothes, they say, make a statement, and in the Philippines this statement may be as political as it is personal. There were times in Philippine history when Filipinos wore clothes in shame or defiance, thus giving political color to this usually apolitical aspect of culture.

Some Indios tried to ape the Spaniards by wearing European coats with tails over tailored trousers. Not wanting to look like the natives, the Spaniards forbade the Indios from tucking their shirts in. Thus, the Indio strutted about in his untucked shirt, looking like a half-dressed European.

During the heady days of the People Power revolution, a sea of yellow-clad civilians surrounded two military camps in Manila. Their yellow headbands, armbands, and hats signaled their support for Cory Aquino (yellow was her prefered color). A small group in green waved a banner with Vice President Salvador Laurel's name. White was for the seminarians and nuns who faced the tanks. On the other side of the city, red and blue floated below the balcony where Ferdinand and Imelda Marcos were singing their last duet on Philippine television.

THE UNBALANCED SOCIAL CLASSES

Four hundred years of colonization have cemented a social structure that can only be described as stratified. Philippine society has been described as a pyramid: the upper 2% representing the elite, the next 10% comprise the fast dwindling middle class, and the impoverished masses make up the wide base. Enclaves like Forbes Park and Dasmariñas Village that rival America's Beverly Hills can lull a newcomer into disbelieving stories about people living in smokey mountains (generic for garbage dumps) or in sewage pipes. While some houses in Manila have gold bathroom fixtures, children of farmhands die of malnutrition. These contradictions are part of the Philippine landscape and have remained an unanswered challenge for its national leaders.

Children foraging for what they can find in the vast garbage dumping area at the Smokey Mountain squatter settlement just north of Manila. The smoke comes from the burning of rubbish along the hill of this dumping site.

THE FILIPINA— HER SOCIAL STATUS AND ROLE

The modern Filipina ("FIL-li-PEEN-nah") has come a long way since the days of ancient priestesses. What she is now is a product of varied influences that include pre-Spanish self-possession, Castilian medieval morality, American individualism, and Chinese enterprise.

In pre-Spanish society, she occupied prestigious positions, including that of the priestess, the central figure of the tribe. When Christianity came, she was placed in a moral straitjacket, the effects of which are felt even to this day. Modern Filipinas still adhere to the Maria Clara ideal—the demure, gentle, pious, malleable woman. Any sign of sexual aggressiveness condemns one to a reputation mothers would cry over. American education taught the Filipina that she too could excel, that she too could nurture ambitions. Today, Filipinas outnumber their male counterparts in universities. They have likewise inched their way into corporate boardrooms and have made their mark in professions previously dominated by men.

A present-day Filipina performs a dual role: the traditional role of daughter, sister, wife, and mother, and the modern role of breadwinner. She continues to perform household and child-rearing chores, even if she runs a multimillion-peso company or harvests rice in the fields. She is closer to her children because of the long years of emotional nurturing they receive from her. In return, the children are loyal to her and look upon her as the greatest influence in their lives. Because she is the emotional center of the family, she wields immense power over the other members, a power she displays only when necessary. Most of the time, she good-naturedly defers to her husband, who enjoys playing the role of the boss.

Women constitute an important part of the workforce and many have found successful careers.

Most wealthy Filipino women help in their husbands businesses or pursue separate careers. Very few educated women opt for the life of a housewife; the easy availability of servants allows them to pursue a career. There are times when they assume the role of breadwinner or earn more than their husbands. In the case of the former, the husband acquiesces since he is probably out of work. In the latter, professional jealousy may erupt since the husband's machismo is challenged by the wife's success.

Filipinas have also done much for nation-building. In the struggle for independence, they acted as keepers of arms, couriers, and social covers for their revolutionary relatives. They helped the wounded, fed the hungry, and sheltered the hunted. One widow, Gabriela Silang, mounted her dead husband's horse and continued to lead his rebellion. In more recent times, an ordinary housewife toppled a feared dictator, who had said that women were only meant for the bedroom; Corazon Aquino became the first woman president of the Philippines.

47

LIFESTYLE

"FILIPINOS," it is said, "are Malay in family, Spanish in love, Chinese in business, and American in ambition." Because they were shaped by 300 years in a Spanish convent and 50 years in Hollywood, Filipinos are considered the least Oriental of all Orientals. Yet this potent combination of Malay warmth, Latin charm, and American tastes makes the Pinoys ("PIN-nois"), the Filipinos' nickname for themselves, a class all their own.

Opposite and below: **The exuberant spirit of the Filipinos and their great creativity and capacity for enjoyment are an innate part of their character.**

ATTITUDES

HIYA One of the keys to the Filipino character is their sense of *hiya,* ("HIH-yah"), meaning "shame," which approximates to the general Asian notion of "face." It refers to the Filipinos' concern for social conformity and suggests their deep immersion in communal tradition. It is also associated with self-esteem, something Filipinos prize above material comfort.

Their estimate of themselves depends on society's estimate of them. Hence, a Filipino who is criticized in public loses social approval and self-esteem and consequently suffers *hiya*. This is why Filipinos react violently to a public insult. Conversely, they will never openly tell others that they smell bad or that they are making fools of themselves for fear of making other people lose their self-esteem.

If Filipinos value their own and their neighbors' "face," they must learn *pakikisama,* the art of smooth interpersonal relationships, in order to succeed in their culture.

"*Pakikisama*" has no exact equivalent in English, but can be roughly defined as "getting along" or submitting to group will.

PAKIKSAMA *Pakikisama* (pa-KI-ki-SUM-mah") is based on the assumption that the community is more important than the individual. Some Filipinos may disagree with the opinion of the majority, but usually they will not express their disagreement as this will go against *pakikisama*. A girl may refuse to go out on a date with a neighbor's son, but she will say that she has to study for an exam rather than cause the neighboring family to lose face and strain relations between their households.

Filipinos dislike confrontations in general and are averse to breaking a congenial atmosphere with dissent. Criticisms are put across through a go-between or through light banter and teasing. They are highly sensitive to social propriety (*delicadeza*) and look down on people who overstay their welcome or who enrich themselves while in a position of power.

Finally, there is the Filipino version of sincerity. Sincerity is not necessarily frankness as the West understands it. To the Filipino, it is being true to society's expectations of him or her. The Filipino "yes" for example is not always a "yes." In order not to cause someone who requests a favor to lose face, Filipinos will say "yes" when actually they mean "no."

If Filipinos do not follow up on invitations, then they have considered the invitations to be only polite gestures and not binding. Filipinos do not mean to lie, they simply do not want to offend the person inviting them by being ungracious.

Some of the Filipinos' strengths may also be weaknesses. They can be the most hospitable hosts in the world. They would give their best food and best bed to a visitor, welcome or otherwise. Colonizers read this as a sign of servility and inferiority. Moreover, Filipinos have a strong sense of fatalism that has enabled them to weather all forms of disasters but has ironically also prevented them from controlling their destiny.

FILIPINO HUMOR

Generally, Filipinos approach life with a sense of fun. Their *joie de vivre* is so great that foreigners think that Filipinos seem to be laughing at something all the time. Nothing is sacred to Filipinos, not even themselves. They poke fun at anything that catches their fancy— their neighbor's curtains, the latest fashion, movie idols, a First Lady's predilection for kitsch, their empty wallets. Even in their darkest hour, the Filipinos turn to humor and thereby keep their sanity.

Laughter and humor is an irrepressible part of the Filipino make-up.

Imagine someone dressed to the hilt making a grand entrance in a party. Suddenly he slips and falls flat on his face. What does he do? He stands up, smiles and challenges his audience: *"O, kaya ba ninyo iyan?"* ("Can you follow that?")—humor saves his face.

Humor can also be political. More than the speeches of the opposition, it was the Marcos and Ninoy jokes that appealed to the people in 1986. Exposing issues became a cinch through jokes. A typical example involves the use of pun: *"Marcos, ano ang problema ng bayan? Kapitalismo, Pyudalismo, Imperialismo, Ikaw mismo!"* ("Marcos, what are the problems of the country? Capitalism, Feudalism, Imperialism, Yourself!")

Catastrophes are borne with grace when taken with a sense of humor. Floods, typhoons, and earthquakes lose their ability to dampen the spirit when seen in a humorous light. A girl pinned by a slab of concrete that fell during an earthquake had her spirits kept up by a rescue worker's unceasing chatter on how best to cook noodles.

Some 10 million people live in Metro Manila, a sprawling metropolis comprising 13 municipalities. The metropolis' charm and vitality reflect its multifaceted heritage and the freewheeling spirit of its people.

COSMOPOLITAN MANILA

Images of Manila can only be described as "melange, baroque, eclectic, hodgepodge, collage, potpourri … chop suey."

Sixteenth century churches blend with skyscrapers; Chinese spring rolls are dipped in vinegar and garlic, not in soy sauce. American pop serves as background for Filipino tearjerkers; Chinatown *karaoke* joints play Spanish love songs. Before a red light, a BMW stops alongside a tricycle (the Filipino trishaw), while street children peer through the car windows begging. Politicians meet in a coffee shop to discuss the next elections, while outside, demonstrators hurl rocks at the riot policemen. A typhoon comes and classes are suspended—movie houses make a killing. Even during the harshest times, the Manileños never forget to have a good time. They are perpetually on the lookout for the best restaurants, the latest disco, and the trendiest fashion. A young man will brave the rush hour traffic and the pickpocket, and break a date with his girlfriend in order not to miss a basketball game on television, where he can see his favorite cager make a three-point basket.

THE COUNTRYSIDE

Life in the *barrio* ("BAH-rio") or village is not measured in terms of hours but of seasons—planting, harvesting, milling, and planting again. Time passes so slowly that change is hardly noticed. Telephones are practically non-existent, although TV and radio sets are common. With a number of overseas workers coming from the barrios, a few households have acquired video sets, not for private enjoyment but for communal pleasure. The owner rents a tape from the township, and at night neighbors come to watch for a minimal fee. Since doctors are hardly present in the villages, people seek the services of an herb doctor or a faith healer. An elementary school may be available to the children, but older students may have to walk miles to get to a high school. The center of activity in the neighborhood is the *sari-sari* ("sah-REE SAH-ree") store, the local sundry shop, where not only money and goods are exchanged but also the latest gossip.

People in the countryside like doing things together, from washing clothes in the river to planting rice or building houses. Backyards are shared and fences are built only to separate houses from the roads, not from the occupant. The neighbor's tree is considered one's own. Only those from the city would think that taking a fruit from it is stealing.

The neighborhood store is often a good place to while away an afternoon.

A fisherman's family on Simunul Island, Tawi-Tawi, forms the basic social unit of a society where kinship ties are all important.

KINSHIP TIES

As far as Filipino relationships are concerned, that of the family is the most basic, the strongest, and the most enduring. The family consists of the father, mother, and siblings, but it can extend to very distant relatives as well as close friends and loyal servants. The *compadrazgo* ("COM-pud-DRAS-co") system brings non-blood relations into the family and enables the poor peasant to establish kinship ties with the richest people in the village.

The Filipino is never seen as an individual but as part of a family or community. Everyone belongs to someone or something and identity is established and desired, based on the kinship group. During social occasions, for instance, one remains a stranger until one's kinship group is determined; only after mutual relatives, friends, officemates, or townmates have been dug up can interaction flow smoothly.

Independence is not a primary value and going it alone is simply seen as disliking one's family. An adult who continues to live with parents is hardly considered weak or spineless; at times, he or she may be considered devoted.

Strong kinship ties are the Filipinos' best coping mechanism during critical times; they offer a strong support system that never fails to pull people through. However, these ties are also a social bane. Corporate and political nepotism can be rationalized as being helpful to one's family. Often, Filipinos are torn between their official duties and their kinship obligations. This contradiction and duality is very much a part of Filipino life and society.

BIRTH

Birth is usually an occasion everyone welcomes. There is much speculation with regard to the baby's sex and name and who it takes after. In fact, in some offices, betting on the sex of the pregnant colleague's baby can cause hilarious moments.

In the rural areas, most babies are delivered at home. The placenta is buried beneath the house, often with an object symbolizing what the parents want the child to be. In the cities, this practice is prohibited by health authorities.

The first religious ritual for a child is Baptism, when he or she becomes a Christian. For the occasion, the parents invite sponsors to be the godparents of the child. The godparents' task is to take over the rearing of the child if the parents are no longer able and to look after and advise the godchild on how to deal with a harsh environment. This system, called *compadrazgo,* assures the child's social and financial future.

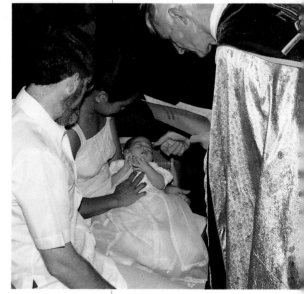

A Baptismal ceremony.

*The Filipino child
is never alone.... .
Since the child is
in such
continuing
contact with
others, he or she
develops a good
many techniques
for handling the
variety of stresses
which inevitably
arise.*

THE GROWING UP YEARS

Child rearing in the Philippines is a communal affair. From the time Filipinos are born, they are handled with solicitude and tenderness by family members and friends. They are never alone while growing up. They are constantly surrounded, if not by siblings, then by other relatives. They are taught the value of smooth interpersonal relationships at an early age and get to practice it first within the family. Filipino parents are generally unhurried and undemanding in the training of children, but they are particular in cultivating obedience and concern for others.

Children are essential in any social gathering; very often they are obliged to perform for their elders. This is probably why so many Filipinos are good musicians and performers.

No great ceremony attends the onset of puberty for boys and girls. Village boys go to the local barber or herb doctor and prove their manhood by being circumcised without anesthesia. Those in the cities do it in a more clinical and painless way. When girls first menstruate, they are simply taught hygiene and are advised about proper decorum. They are also warned of hungry wolves outside who must not be provoked by wanton behavior.

COURTSHIP

Traditional courtship in the Philippines reflects Hispanic influence in its manner and morality. A young man paying court at a young woman's house has to contend with her relatives who will ply him with questions. If he asks her out, she will have to bring along a chaperon. Chaperons may be dispensed with during group dates, but curfews are maintained. A young man may woo his heart's desire with flowers and candy, but she may show disinterest as befits a

A young woman being courted could find herself being serenaded by a suitor, who may bring with him a group of friends to provide the music and the camaraderie.

well-bred young lady. She may cruelly ignore him at first to test his tenacity and sincerity. In the countryside, a young man may show interest in a girl by serenading her. Accompanied by friends, he sings beneath her window on a moonlit night.

Modern courtships allow solo dates and candlelight dinners, but premarital sex is frowned upon. The younger set may go to a disco or a rock concert for dates but is nonetheless reminded to behave properly in public.

Bridesmaids await their turn to do their part at a wedding ceremony at the San Agustin Church in Manila. Wedding ceremonies can sometimes be elaborate affairs involving entourages of bridesmaids, maids-of-honor, and flower girls.

MARRIAGE

In the Philippines, marriage is by choice but family approval is sought. A man signifies his desire to marry a woman by formally asking for her hand. The practice, called *pamanhikan* ("PAH-man-HE-khan"), may be initiated by a go-between who is a mutual relative or acquaintance of both families. The wishes of the couple may or may not count, depending on the graciousness of both sets of parents. It is traditionally the groom's family who shoulders the wedding expenses. Amidst the *pamanhikan* feast, the date, time, church, sponsors, and reception are settled.

The wedding itself, simple or grand, is celebrated in church after which a reception follows. In some areas, the wedding reception includes a dance during which relatives and friends of the newlyweds pin money on the dancing couple. The length of paper money running from their shoulders to the ground indicates the financial standing of the families; the amount the couple collects should be enough to start them out in life.

DEATH

As in birth, death is never an individual burden or loss. As soon as a death is announced, relatives and friends come to mourn with the bereaved family. They are received warmly and told the circumstances of death while they partake of food and drinks. While a sense of loss pervades a wake, no one is required to be grave. A wake is very often a reunion of seldom-seen relatives and friends and may take the semblance of a fiesta. Immediate

family living overseas are obliged to come home, which lends joy to an otherwise sad affair. Night vigils are a must, and relatives and friends take turns keeping the bereaved family company. In the countryside, people have poetic jousts and games to keep themselves awake. Neither a sign of disrespect nor callousness, this festivity is meant to help the family forget their sorrow for a while.

While sending wreaths is customary, most people feel that giving money to help defray an expensive funeral service is more practical. When the deceased is finally buried, overt grief is expected of the family. Husband and wife may have hated each other when alive, but any self-respecting husband or wife will cry at a spouse's funeral or even faint at the burial. The dead are always remembered in the Philippines. A nine-day novena is held for the deceased after the burial and death anniversaries are celebrated with a Mass or a visit to the grave.

The vast majority of Filipinos are Christians and are given a Christian burial in the town cemeteries. On All Saints Day, Filipinos troop to the cemeteries to honor their dead relatives.

RELIGION

ANCIENT FILIPINOS believed that the world was controlled by spirits that manifested themselves through nature. Even today, they conduct rituals to ask for rain from the rain god or a bountiful harvest from the earth god. Rocks, trees, and animals are likewise worshiped. A universal god called Bathala rules the cosmos and decides human fate. The spirits of ancestors called *anitos* are also venerated and can be appealed to for guidance and protection. While an individual can pray directly to the gods, prayers are more easily heard when passed through the gods' spokeswoman, the priestess.

CHRISTIANITY AND FOLK CATHOLICISM

The missionaries arrived filled with the zeal to save the pagan souls of the natives. They built impressive churches and preached the virtuous path to salvation. However, the philosophy of the medieval Castilian religion was alien to the natives' world view, and the priests despaired that once their backs were turned the natives' frequently returned to old practices. The Christian religion was imposed, but it would be inaccurate to say that the Filipino accepted the whole European Catholic structure. Historians seem to see not the Christianizing of a people, but that of a people's practices and rituals. Christianity in the Philippines has many pagan beliefs that make it unique to Filipino culture.

61

Christianity and Folk Catholicism

Opposite: **A mass tribal communion and holy rites at Santa Cruz Mission, Mindanao.**

Below: **Enshrined in almost every household, the Santo Niño (Holy Child) statue comes in varying images.**

One easily discerns this in the manner people practice the religion. A good example is the strong devotion to Mary and the Child Jesus. Nowhere else in the world does one see the Virgin in various functions, such as protector during a voyage, as a shield against foreign invasion, or even as a fertility deity. Children often call her Mama Mary. And nowhere else does one see cults devoted solely to the Infant Jesus, where he is bathed, fed, clothed in rich brocade, and treated as a princely guest in a house. Over 50 icons of the Virgin and the Child Jesus in the Philippines are said to be miraculous, several of them recognized by the Church as authentic sources of miracles. Another example is the veneration of saints for ensuring good harvests, for bringing rain, for finding the right spouse, for begetting children, and for answering a host of secular needs. Christian sacraments and prayers are mystical rituals not unlike ancient rituals of supplication and incantation. The friar may have merely supplanted the priestess as spiritual go-between.

Filipinos take their faith seriously. It is their source of strength in times of trouble. They believe divine guidance is the reason for their accomplishments. Their mystical nature does not distinguish between the sources of these beliefs. What is important is that something more powerful than themselves turns the wheel of life and may be counted on for help.

CHRISTIAN RITUALS

Baptism, being the first ritual in a person's life, is accorded great importance. The rites of Confirmation and First Communion further strengthen the tie between the believer and his faith. The transition to responsible adulthood is often marked by matrimony. The final ritual is ended with the last sacrament administered to a dying person. Everyday rituals include Masses or services, novenas, processions, family rosaries, the angelus, and grace before meals. Special rituals are performed on special religious events such as the *visita iglesia* (literally, "visiting churches") on Holy Thursday, the blessing of fire and wood on Black Saturday, the midnight Mass on Christmas Eve, abstinence from eating

In a country rife with faith and fanaticism, religious processions such as this are a common sight.

meat on all Lenten Fridays, offering of flowers to the Virgin in May, and others. Christian blessings are given to a new building, a new house, a new vehicle, a new restaurant or boutique before it can be used or occupied.

OTHER FAITHS

The Philippines is 93% Christian, the only Christian nation in Asia. Believers of other faiths, however, are free to practice their religions. Islam came earlier than Christianity but was contained because of colonization. It is now concentrated in southern Mindanao. Taoist and Buddhist worship flourishes amidst countless Chinese communities thoughout the country. Monks are even imported to man the temples and lead the rituals. The Hindus and Sikhs form a small minority and have their own religious enclaves.

A mosque in downtown Manila. Manila during the mid-16th century was a Moslem city-state until the arrival of the Spanish. Moslems today form the largest minority in the Philippines.

THE CATHOLIC CHURCH

In the Philippines, almost every *barangay* has a church or a chapel. In some parts of Manila and in most of the countryside, churches date back to the 16th or 17th century, products of the religious zeal of the missionaries and the ingenuity and artistry of local craftsmen. A Catholic church usually has a squarish nave, a bell tower, and the priest's residence at the side or behind the church proper. It was built to withstand typhoons and fires but unfortunately, not earthquakes. (San Agustin, the oldest church, was severely damaged by earthquake several times, burying both priests and parishioners in the rubble.) The church contains a central altar, but may have side altars where statues of saints are enshrined. The bell tower is traditionally a measure of a church's prosperity, but more than that, the bell serves as an alarm system (against attacking pirates) or a public information system (it announces deaths, baptisms, weddings), aside from being a people's call to Mass.

FAITH HEALING

Faith healing is the act of curing simply by prayer or by touch, without the aid of implements or drugs. The practice existed in the Philippines even before the advent of medical science and has been the domain of the *babaylan* ("BY-BY-lun") and later the herb doctor. Progress did not kill it, but modernized it. Due to high medical costs, poor people still turn to the faith healer, who normally does not charge lest he lose his power.

Today's faith healers need not be pagan nor unschooled. They claim to be guided by Christian deities and may even have a measure of medical know-how.

Faith healing comes in different forms. The most simple is healing by prayer whereby the healer ejects the spirits of disease through the force of prayer. Some healers lay hands upon the body of the sick person or make use of herbal concoctions, oils, and incantations. Most cure while in a trance. The most dramatic and most controversial is psychic surgery, which is the process of opening up human bodies and extracting tumors or diseased parts simply by the hands. No anesthesia is used because no pain is felt. The patient can go disco dancing the next day if he or she wants to.

Reports of success have given rise to debates. Unconvinced medical doctors claim it is all a sham, that the psychic surgeon conceals in his hand a bloodied cotton ball, and that the extracted tissue is actually a chicken's or a pig's liver. Nonetheless, how can one argue with a woman whose uterine tumor has disappeared as attested by her gynecologist? Or with a

Herbal medicines such as these, ranging from leaves, barks, and twigs to various oils culled from local plants, are used by herb doctors to cure all forms of ailments.

nun who swears by the Holy Spirit that her hemorrhoids were cured? Is it possible that spiritual power can open and close the body without pain or blood, or that molecules can be arranged in a few minutes?

Shaman or sham, the faith healer remains a recourse as long as people believe.

ANTING-ANTING

The Filipino amulet or talisman called *anting-anting* ("UN-ting Un-ting") is often a combination of Christian and pagan elements. Serving mainly to ward off evil, to acquire invulnerability, and to secure business luck, the *anting-anting* may contain the picture of a saint plus Latin inscriptions, and will be kept along with a crocodile's tooth, tree bark, and pig's hair. Some are worn like medals; others are swallowed or are unseen.

The most popular way to acquire extraordinary power, it is said, is to set out at midnight on Black Saturday and look for a banana blossom about to open. When it does, it ejects a dew-like teardrop called *mutya* that you catch in your mouth. You will then see evil spirits around you and wrestle with them until Easter dawn. If you live through that, you will acquire supernatural powers and become invulnerable.

Amulets can be passed on to younger relatives. Sick people who take a long time to die are allegedly in possession of an amulet that they must pass on in order to expire.

The *anting-anting* is part of history too. More than once, men thought they possessed its powers and rushed toward guns, armed only with a cross or a *bolo*. They were convinced that the bullets would bounce off. They did not.

In the Philippines there is an incredible mixture of Christian and local folk beliefs such as those that have surrounded the cult of the Child Jesus or Holy Child.

FOLK BELIEFS

Early Filipinos believed in a soul and an afterlife. Death was simply a change in form; the dead person carried on with his or her usual activities in the spirit world. The Bagobos of southeastern Mindanao believe in the existence of two souls within the person, one good and one evil. The Bukidnon believe there are seven souls within a person that merge and migrate to Mount Balatocan upon death. Most acknowledge the possibility of spirits coming back so they have created prayers and rituals that will lead the spirit to the world where it belongs.

The reality of life after death was reinforced by Christianity, and it is therefore not strange to find Christian elements in what are supposed to be pagan beliefs. For example, pagan creatures of the underworld (not Christian inventions) are subdued by a cross or holy water. Christianity does acknowledge and thus cannot stem beliefs in fairies, elves, hexes and spells, nocturnal creatures of the earth, and ghosts.

Filipinos also acknowledge the unseen. For instance, when someone is walking along they will often say *"Tabi tabi po"* ("Excuse me, please step aside") for fear of stepping on an unseen elf. A pregnant woman is not to be left alone or a hungry spirit or *asuang* ("AH-swung") may eat her baby. A child's sudden and unexplained illness could have been caused by an earth spirit who took a fancy to him or her. Thus, a herb doctor is summoned and deciphers what happened by melting candle wax on water until figures emerge.

These examples highlight not so much Filipino imagination but the Filipinos' recognition of worlds other than theirs, and their willingness to straddle the fence between scientific logic and folk beliefs.

MYTHS AND LEGENDS

Myths are created in order to make sense of the world in a manner that one understands. Based on their world view and environment, early Filipinos tried to answer the most fundamental question of human origins by weaving their creation myths.

The first Filipino man and woman.

A bird pecked at the bamboo until it split open, and the first man and woman, the first Filipino parents, emerged. Some versions say that they were siblings, forced to mate in order to propagate the world. Another legend says there were two bamboos from which each emerged without the knowledge of the other. They met, married, and bore children. Belief in a bird as the creature who unlocked human life suggests an ancient reverence for birds. The Tagalogs identify one bird with their chief god, Bathala. Legends trace origins of things. According to a northern Luzon legend, the sky used to be low, but a maiden pounded her rice so vigorously that her wooden pole pushed up the sky. Her jewelry, which she hung on the clouds, now twinkles as stars. Legends also help give concrete shape to an ideal, as in the case of the virtuous Mariang Makiling, the famous *diwata* ("dee-WAT-ta"), meaning fairy or goddess, of Laguna who inspired the young Rizal. She fell in love with a mortal who took advantage of her goodness. As a result, she vanished from human sight forever.

LANGUAGE

THE PHILIPPINES has more than 80 languages and dialects, nine of which serve as major languages and are spoken by 89% of the population. While all belong to the Malayo-Polynesian family, the languages are different enough to make it impossible for the speaker of one language to understand the speaker of another.

FILIPINO

Filipino, which is Tagalog-based, is the Philippine national language. It is spoken by people in the Metro Manila area as well as the southern Luzon Tagalog provinces and is understood by 90% of the population. It is slowly becoming the language of instruction and, as stated in the 1987 Constitution, will eventually become the official language of the government.

Opposite: **Philippine languages are steeped in courtesy. Here, two oarsman take respite from work while exchanging pleasantries.**

Left: **A movie billboard in Filipino, the national language. Differences in the languages spoken in the Philippines have resulted in the introduction of a national language to transcend the problem of communication across languages.**

FOREIGN TONGUES

English is the widest used foreign language in the Philippines simply because it has been the language of instruction for almost eight decades. At present, it is still the language of instruction for higher education and is still largely the language of the government and mass media. People who speak different regional languages may converse with each other in English. Filipinos speak a variety of English culled mainly from the United States that has been infused with the idiosyncracies of the native language or dialect. In informal situations, people often use a combination of languages resulting in what is called Taglish (Tagalog-English).

Before 1987, Spanish was a required subject in school. At present, Spanish speakers have become rare, although most Filipinos have a working knowledge of the language. Filipino, the language, is liberally laced with Spanish words.

Hokkien or Fujianese is mostly spoken by the Philippine Chinese and has contributed substantially to Philippine languages in terms of vocabulary. Indian influences can be seen in the ancient scripts as well as loan words.

NAMES: A MERRY MIX

Most Filipinos bear Iberian-sounding surnames, but this does not mean Iberian ancestry. This was the result of a Spanish decree in the 19th century which required all natives to acquire a Spanish surname for easier identification. In fact, in many Philippine towns, surnames begin with the same letter. The decree gave surnames beginning with A to the capital and B, C and others to the outlying towns. It was, therefore, easy to trace one's municipal origins using this method. The choice of first names, however, was dictated by one's birth. One was named after the saint whose feast day falls on one's birthday. Priests would not baptize someone unless they were named after a saint.

When Filipinos started to use English names, it became more complicated. No one has heard of St. Peggy or St. Susie. A happy compromise then was to affix the word "Maria" (for the Virgin Mary) to Peggy or Susie. This is so common that 50% of Filipina girls seem to have been named Maria. The fad for nicknames followed. Milagros finds her name old-fashioned, so she prefers to be called Mila or Mimi; Antonio becomes Tony and Jose becomes Jojo or Joey. A variety of influences can be seen in a name like Jose Bayani Chan—JB to his friends.

Tagalog speakers, the second largest linguistic and cultural group in the Philippines, number at least 10 million people, and are located in central Luzon (including Manila) and parts of Mindanao.

WHEN THE BODY SPEAKS

BODY CONTACT Because of their warm nature, Filipinos like to touch. There is much physical contact among relatives and close friends. Greetings can be made by *mano* ("MAHN-no") meaning "hand," a gesture of respect when a young person puts the back of the hand of an older person on their forehead, by kissing the cheek of relatives, or by *beso-beso* ("BAE-so BAE-so"), meaning "kiss-kiss." *Beso-beso* is a cheek-to-cheek greeting among women or among friends, including those of the opposite sex. More conservative girls, however, will be content with a handshake.

SAYING IT WITH THE EYEBROWS Filipinos say an unspoken hello by simply lifting the eyebrows. The lift must not be too long or the gesture turns into a query.

GESTURES OF HOSTILITY Staring is a gesture of provocation and may cause undue harm to the curious. Arms akimbo is a gesture of arrogance and should only be seen in a teacher reprimanding a pupil or a policeman confiscating a license.

GESTURES OF RESPECT Greeting a superior can take the form of a nod. When walking between two people in conversation, one says, "Excuse me" and bows, extending the hand as one walks between them. To catch the attention of another person, one never shouts or beckons with a finger. Instead, try to catch his or her eye and signal with a nod or with a hand, palm facing downward.

THE SMILE A Filipino does everything with a smile—he praises with a smile, criticizes with a smile, condoles with a smile, takes life's trials with

Above: The *mano*, a traditional way of greeting elders and the *beso-beso*.

a smile. A confrontation is best avoided but when unavoidable is begun with a smile. A smile can be sheepish when someone wants something from you, or it can be sarcastic when you are about to be scolded. Embarrassing moments are covered with smiles, while allegations are refuted with a knowing grin.

ARTS

WHILE ANCIENT PHILIPPINE LITERATURE took the form of oral stories such as myths, legends, and folktales that were closely interwoven into the people's lives, Christianity brought a religious-based literature that consisted of morality and passion plays as well as stories based on the life of the saints. Because Filipinos were barred from the classroom, their reading material was mainly dictated by the church.

By the 18th and 19th centuries, however, a group of Filipinos had acquired education and started to write both in the vernacular and in Spanish. One of the important writings of this era is Francisco Baltazar's *Florante at Laura,* a Tagalog narrative in verse. Intellectuals educated in Europe wrote anti-Spanish, anti-clergy texts, not with a Filipino audience in mind but a Spanish one. The greatest works of the period, and perhaps in all of Philippine literary history, are the novels of José Rizal, *Noli me Tangere* (1912) and *El Filibusterismo* (1912), both realistic depictions of Spanish abuses and Filipino nationalistic aspirations.

The coming of the Americans gave birth to a literature in English. Barely 20 years after the first class in English was set up, the first short story was published. Although the first attempts were awkward, literature in English has since then achieved greater heights, as can be seen in the volume of work published from 1920 to the present.

The 50s and early 60s were the golden age of writing in English. This period saw the simultaneous publication of writers such as NVM González, Francisco Arcellana, Bienvenido Santos, F. Sionil José, and of course, Nick Joaquín, the most famous of them all. Two schools of thought emerged with the development of writing in English. They were the art for art's sake

Opposite: **A Goddess of Fertility painting on a house ceiling in Bulacan Province, Central Luzon.**

Above: **José Rizal's** *El Filibusterismo*—**powerful social literature of the time.**

group, led by poet José Garcia Villa, and those who were convinced by Salvador López's essay *Literature and Society* that literature should be a mirror of society.

The issue was extended to the use of English, viewed by some writers as a colonial language. With the surge of nationalism in the 60s and 70s, many writers have shifted to Filipino as a medium, and writers in the regional languages were given their due importance. Social realism has become a strong contemporary tradition.

Filipinos are great followers of popular culture. They may like Shakespeare, but that does not mean they don't love comics, too. *Sari-sari* stores often rent comics so people can follow their favorite serials.

The average Filipino is not averse to popular literature. Comic stands such as this provide hours of reading pleasure, and an escape from the humdrum.

DANCE

Filipino dances reflect Malay and Spanish influences. The *singkil* ("SING-kil") danced by a graceful Filipina between bamboo poles never fails to elicit raves from audiences. The *jota* ("HOR-tah") and *curacha* ("koo-RAH-chah") of Spain are the highlight of school programs and fiestas. Indigenous dances recreate nature (the movement of birds and fowl, for instance), celebrate a warrior's victory, re-enact courtship, or mourn a death. The famous Filipino bamboo dance, the *tinikling* ("tin-NICK-ling"), copies the agile movements of a bird as it traipses along the reeds. Ballet thrives and is given support and exposure when funds are available. Modern dance has its niche at the Cultural Center in Manila. Nowhere in the world can one see so many dance performances and contests as on Philippine television. Trained in his or her living room, the Filipino will never miss a village dance or a disco on a Saturday night.

The *singkil*, a folk dance of Moslem origin.

MUSIC

To say that Filipinos are a musical people is to dilute a cliché. For Filipinos, singing is like breathing, one of the essential things in life ....

If there is anything Filipinos should be proud about, it is the international recognition given their musical talents. As with dance, they also trained at home, and whatever musical talents they have are further honed in the numerous programs they have to participate in at school and at parties. No fiesta is ever complete without the amateur singing contest; swankier versions exist on Philippine television, some programs even running for decades.

Contemporary Filipino music is basically Western in sound and even in language, but the sentimentality, the inclination to romantic subjects, and the mellow sound are Filipino. Although translations of English songs

One of Philippines' best-known folk singers, Freddie Aguilar, in concert. Music permeates all aspects of Filipino life.

abound, more discerning listeners are opting for original compositions, especially those written in Filipino. Philippine airwaves are dominated by American rock and pop, but all stations are now required to play Filipino tunes every hour. Filipino musicians are in demand anywhere in the world, but the best are still in the country. Concerts and live acts are a staple in the local music scene. Clubs of all kinds—folk, jazz, rock-and-roll—cater to all kinds of musical taste.

Classical music is considered highbrow but is highly patronized nevertheless. Performances are held in the Cultural Center, the Metropolitan theater or the PCI Bank auditorium. Scholarships sponsored by other countries have been won easily and protegées have brought honor to the Philippines by their triumphs abroad.

Ethnic music is still played in the tribal communities. Instruments include Moslem gongs (the *kulintangan*), the Apayao bamboo guitar, the local Jew's harp, called the *kubing,* and the bamboo nose flute. There have been efforts to preserve ethnic music in its pristine state, but there are also those who wish to incorporate it into contemporary life by using ethnic instruments in local pop compositions.

That all Filipinos can sing may be a myth, but that all Filipinos appreciate music is not far from the truth.

Above: **Indigenous musical instruments, such as the *kulintang* and the *kubing,* are used in the tribal communities.**

Below: **The *tuba,* a Western import, is played during fiestas and public holidays.**

The *cenaculo,* a distinctly Filipino version of the Passion Play, is staged in many villages and towns during Holy Week. It is dramatic and highly stylized.

DRAMA

Early Philippine drama was performed as part of the rituals that accompanied activities such as planting and harvesting as well as birth and death. Like literature, drama was enmeshed in everyday life and did not need a stage or lights.

European drama came as part of the evangelization process. Passion and morality plays were encouraged. The *cenaculo* ("si-NAH-KU-loh"), a play on the life of Christ, is still performed today. Secular drama came in the form of the *comedia* or *moro-moro,* which depicted the Christians' victory over the Moors, and the *zarzuela,* which combined theater and music. During the early part of the American occupation, seditious *zarzuelas* were performed to protest at colonial exploitation.

Dramas in English were first seen at the universities. Favored topics were historical events and domestic problems. In the late 60s, with the resurgence of nationalism, dramas in English gave way to a new batch of writers who used Filipino. At the height of activism, there was renewed interest in drama, which was seen as the most potent art form for exposition of national issues. At present, drama continues to thrive. Performances are often world-class. The drama in Filipino has arrived even while plays in English continue to be written. Foreign classical plays are staged by university groups, while contemporary Western plays and musicals are staples of professional theater groups.

FILM, PAINTING, AND SCULPTURE

As far as the ordinary Filipino is concerned, the world outside is what one sees in the movies. Hollywood has shaped the Filipino mind for so long that Filipinos have begun to believe that there are cowboys in the Cordillera mountains. There was a local Elvis Presley who even imitated Elvis' pelvis; there was a local James Dean and a John Travolta. In the tradition of Hollywood, Filipino movies are full of sex and violence. Fortunately, a concerned group of directors have persevered in creating quality films that have not only tackled the realities of Philippine life but also brought out the best in Filipino cinematic artistry.

Painting and sculpture have been largely influenced by the West. The first distinguished painters, Juan Luna and Felix Resurrecion Hidalgo, won awards in Spain and Paris. Modern painters and sculptors continue to produce a wide mix of art forms in traditional or experimental themes and techniques.

A portrait of a lady by Juan Luna, who won the most prestigious international art award of the time, the Prix de Rome. He and his compatriot, Felix Resurrecion Hidalgo, brought world acclaim for Filipino artists.

ART AND CRAFT

Despite the almost total destruction of Philippine pre-Spanish culture, a great deal of craft work has been preserved, especially by those who resisted colonization. Basketry, for example, is highly developed among the Mountain province, Mindanao, and Mindoro/Palawan tribes. Used to catch fish or store grain and goods, the baskets are woven with such skill and artistry that they now grace the houses of the rich.

Textile weaving is also an indigenous art. The T'boli people dye the bark of a tree and weave the strands into geometric designs. The Yakans produce a flame of colors in their work. Woodcarving and furniture making have produced the most intricate of creations from Philippine trees. The whole town of Paete, Laguna, has made woodcarving a town industry. The town of Betis, Pampanga, has the highest reputation in wooden furniture. Other handicrafts that have put the Philippines on the map are the shellcraft of Cebu and the silver filigree of Baguio.

LEISURE

FILIPINO CHILDREN have few toys but many playmates. The fact that they are usually surrounded by hordes of relatives and friends and that they cannot afford to buy toys makes their play more socially- and game-oriented. To pass time, they go to their backyards or streets to indulge in an hour of hide-and-seek, blind man's buff, *luksong-tinik* (jumping over a stick or outstretched hands), *sungka* (shells or stones put into holes), *siklot* (a local version of jacks), *sipa* (kicking a palm or paper ball), or kite flying.

Opposite and below: **Whether it is spending an evening out at a concert in the park or watching a rodeo competition, Filipinos love to be entertained.**

Adults on the other hand get engrossed in a game of chess or *mahjong,* a game of Chinese origin. Women in the rural areas may play a round of bingo while waiting for the food to cook.

Fiestas are not complete without special games such as the *juego de anillo* (a child tries to hook a ring while riding on a bicycle), the *palo sebo* (a bamboo pole with reward money at the top is greased; children step on each other's bodies to reach the top), cracking-the-pot (blindfolded players try to hit a hanging pot with a pole), and the sack race.

Animal competition is just as popular. Carabao- and horse-fighting are held in some parts of the Philippines, but the most popular animal sport, which has become an institution in Philippine life, is cockfighting.

COCKFIGHTING

Cockfighting is virtually a religion in the islands. Well-heeled businessmen and dirt-poor peasants fill the galleries of cockpits on a Sunday afternoon playing a game of chance with a plumed warrior. Cocks are an owner's prized possession, sometimes considered more important than wives! They are prepared meticulously for the match, massaged and exercised from dawn to dusk.

The match itelf is dominated by a *kristo* ("KRIS-toh"), whose perpetually uplifted hand gives him a Christ-like pose, and who stands at the center, announcing the odds and taking in bets without paper or calculator. Miraculously, he can match bets and faces accurately.

The contest ends when either cock runs away or is unable to fight back. The winning cock must seal his victory by pecking at the losing cock twice. Failure to do so forfeits his victory. Aficionados are passionate about cockfights and will beg, steal, or borrow just to bet on their favorite birds.

SPORTS

Sports in the Philippines vary according to terrain. Land sports include indoor games such as bowling, pelota, boxing, and weightlifting as well as outdoor sports like tennis, volleyball, baseball, jogging, track and field, soccer, and golf. Mountainous regions beckon to the mountain climber and the hang-glider. There are many locations to practice water sports. Swimming, scuba-diving, sailing, windsurfing, and even rowing rate high among the water enthusiasts. However, the Filipino's grand passion in sports is basketball.

Above: **Weightlifting at the CCP Complex, Manila.**

Below: **Windsurfing at Boracay Island resorts.**

BASKETBALL

Basketball is the Filipino's unrequited love. A small guy may dare to venture into a tall man's sport by making up for his shortcomings by being faster and more wily in the hardcourt. But when the crunch comes, it seems that height is still the deciding factor.

Basketball courts are as common as jeepneys in the Philippines. No town plaza or college campus is without a court. Tournaments and sportsfests are opportunities for local talents to show off their skills. Street corners are one-goal courts while mother's flower pot will do just as well.

If there is something parents and children or sweethearts fight about, aside from politics, it is basketball. Philippine Basketball Association

(PBA) teams are objects of admiration and loyalty. On a championship night, everything comes to a standstill as the teams battle for supremacy. The game ends in an exhausting finish, and the fans of the defeated team sigh in dismay as they foresee the ribbing they will get the next day. Since they probably placed large bets on their favorite team, they may end up losing a day's salary, too.

RURAL ENTERTAINMENT

Entertainment in the countryside coincides with the seasons. During the hot summer months, young people look forward to picnics and outdoor dances. When the rains come, they amuse themselves with storytelling or listening to the radio. As soon as they are able, children go out into the streets to play. In most barrios, roads are an extension of the house. On moonlit nights, children play hide-and-seek and other local games.

Religious holidays also provide people with respite from their work in the fields. The most anticipated event, though, is the much celebrated feast day of the patron saint, the town fiesta. The day the carnival comes to town, the town fiesta becomes imminent. Complete with rides, dice games, shooting, and ring booths, the carnival entertains the townspeople for a month or so, answering the need to build up the festive tension until the feast day itself. The celebration then climaxes with brass bands roaming the streets from dawn till dusk, sumptuous meals served in homes and of course, the Mass and the procession that follows.

THE FIESTA

There is no tradition more Filipino than a fiesta. It is a celebration of the pact between the patron saint and the people, with the people thanking the saint for his or her protection. It is a time of baptisms, weddings, and reunions.

Houses are open to everyone, including strangers, and the occasion shows Filipinos at their hospitable best. It is a time for carnivals, games, and beauty contests—a release of the pent-up energy people have been repressing during a year of toil.

A fiesta needs preparation. People spruce up their homes in keeping with the Filipino's concern for appearance. Special food is prepared, for eating is a form of socializing in the country. Even the spirit is prepared.

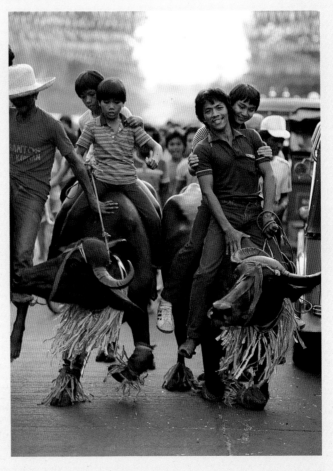

Prior to the fiesta, a nine-day novena is said, capped with a Mass on the feast day itself, celebrated by the bishop, no less. The preparations reach fever pitch as the day draws near, the air electric with anticipation.

On the day itself, people wear their Sunday best. Visitors are advised to eat only a small amount of food in the first house they visit because that is certainly not going to be the last. Wine and goodwill flow freely. The day after, life returns to normal and the poor wonder how to repay the money they borrowed to buy the lavish food they served their guests.

CITY ENTERTAINMENT

Cities offer cosmopolitan pleasures as can be seen in the gigantic shopping malls and the numerous restaurant rows. Nowhere in Asia can you find 12 movie theaters all in one complex and nowhere in Asia can you find tickets so cheap. *Karaoke* litter the streets challenging anyone gutsy enough to take the mike. Discos are there for the nimble-footed. Philippine television offers a host of variety shows and soap operas for the housebound. Manila in particular has various places of interest. The National Museum in Manila and the Ayala Museum in Makati can give one a good introduction to Philippine history and culture.

Opposite: **A water buffalo festival at Bulacan Province, Central Luzon.**

Left: **Discos and music lounges are by far the most popular nightspots in the cities.**

PLACES TO GO

For newcomers, the Philippines offers interesting historical sites that provide a crash course on local history and culture. In Manila, there is Fort Santiago, mute testament to colonial oppression; Casa Manila, a replica of the Spanish *bahay na bato* (stone house); the Rizal Monument at Rizal Park; and relics of contemporary history such as the EDSA marker and the Malacañang Palace museum, where one can enter Imelda Marcos' boudoir.

Outside Manila, there is the Rizal family house in Laguna, the Barosoain church in Bulacan, the Aguinaldo house in Cavite, the Magellan shrine in Cebu, MacArthur's landing spot in Leyte, and Corregidor Island.

If one wants a bird's-eye view of the different regional cultures, one goes to Nayong Pilipino, which contains replicas of important Philippine historical and scenic spots. Paco Park, one of the most pleasant nature-spots in Manila, is the site of many an evening of cultural-musical presentations featuring local and international talents.

NATURE TRIPS

Nature blessed the Philippines with abundance as well as beauty. The weary soul can take refuge in any one of the beautiful beaches around the country. Boracay ("Bur-RAH-kai") in the Visayas is famous for its stretches of white sand and its relative isolation. Batangas, Mindoro, and Pangasinan are for those who have only a few days to spare. El Nido in Palawan is famous for its almost pristine state and its underwater offerings. Pagsanjan ("PUG-sung-hun") in Laguna is noted for its waterfalls as well as its boatmen who deftly negotiate the dangerous rapids. Volcanic springs are popular tourist spots. Baguio is a favorite refuge during the hot months, its air cool and invigorating. Banaue ("Bah-NOW-way"), farther north, brings one to a mountain village where life has remained as simple as it was centuries ago, and a place where one wakes up to the glorious sight of the rice terraces, one of the wonders of the world.

Pagsanjan Falls, two hours south of Manila, offers the memorable boating adventure of going upstream and "shooting the rapids" in a hair-raising run down to the calm waters below.

97

FESTIVALS

THERE ARE FIVE RELIGIOUS EVENTS in Catholic Philippines that are celebrated nationwide:

Holy Thursday, Good Friday, Easter	March/April
All Saints Day	November 1
Christmas	December 25

LENT

Lent, the biggest religious event in the country, commemorates the death and resurrection of Christ. Although mortality is the theme of the occasion, color and drama lighten an otherwise somber affair. Filled with folk rituals and Christian beliefs, the season of Lent begins with Ash Wednesday when crosses of ash are daubed on the foreheads of Catholics.

Opposite: **The annual Moriones Festival in Mogpog town, Marinduque Island, is a spectacular Easter fiesta where participants called *Ma-riones* (which means "plumed helmet" in Spanish) wander the streets of Marinduque clad in Roman soldiers' costumes and wearing bizarre-looking masks with thick beards.**

Left: **Palm leaves are brought to the church to be blessed on Palm Sunday. The long-stalked leaves symbolize the triumphant entry of Jesus Christ into Jerusalem before He was crucified—an event that ushers in the Holy Week.**

Barefooted and shirtless, flagellants, bleeding from self-inflicted beatings, walk the sun-beaten roads.

The climax of the season is Holy Week, which commemorates the week of Christ's death and resurrection. Palm Sunday ushers in Holy Week. Simulating Christ's entry to Jerusalem, people make palm fronds into various designs to be blessed by the priest. These blessed palms are later used to ward off lightning or to cure minor illnesses. During Holy Week, the life and teachings of Christ are chanted in a ritual called the *pabasa* ("pa-BAH-sa"). Flagellants beat their bare backs with glass-spiked leather thongs, not as an act of masochism but in fulfillment of a *panata*, a vow. These men vowed they would undergo the pain and humiliation of this *penitencia* if their requests were granted or if their wrongs were forgiven. Some even go to the extent of having themselves tied or nailed to a cross on Good Friday. An air of gloom descends on the land on Good Friday. At mid-afternoon, the seven last words of Christ are spoken and explained in the pulpits. In the evening, Christ's bier is taken around the town in a procession. At Easter dawn, the *salubong* (meeting) is reenacted. Two carriages carrying the risen Christ and the *Mater Dolorosa* (Grieving Mother) are taken to opposite parts of town. They are to meet at an assigned place called Galilea, a platform where children dressed as angels sing as they lift the mourning veil from the Virgin. The two carriages are then brought back to the church amidst the joyous pealing of bells.

CHRISTMAS

Christmas in the Philippines begins with the first carol played over the radio, that is, sometime in late October. From then on, classrooms, offices, and homes begin to look festive with tinsel and ribbons, Christmas trees and lights. A replica of the Nativity scene complete with shepherds and kings is set up. By the window hangs the *parol,* the Filipino lantern, either in a riot of colors made the Pampango way or in the shape of a star.

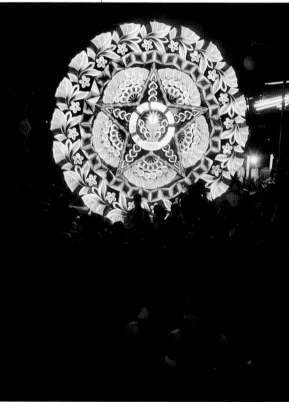

A giant lantern lights up San Fernando town in Pampanga Province on Christmas Eve. It is here that the most spectacular Lantern Festival is held.

Nine dawn Masses precede Christmas Day and while rising early is difficult, the rice cakes one eats after the Mass more than make up for it. Preparations are frenetic on Christmas Eve because the family gathers to eat a sumptuous meal after the midnight Mass. On Christmas morning, children wake up to gifts from Santa Claus. In a Bulacan town, Mary and Joseph's search for a place to stay is reenacted in a ritual called *panunuluyan.* They go from house to house, are turned away and finally find shelter in church.

HONORING PATRON SAINTS

Almost all *barangay* and towns celebrate a fiesta, but there are some fiestas that are more famous than most. In Manila, the most well-known is the feast of the Nazarene, patron saint of Manila's oldest and central district of Quiapo. In January, thousands of devotees clog the main roads of Quiapo in a body-to-body procession led by male devotees, called *hijo* (sons), who pull the carriage of Nuestro Padre Senor Nazareno. The Nazarene has allegedly turned dark because of the constant libation of native perfume. A devotee pushes through a sea of human bodies to wipe a cloth or handkerchief on the face or hands of the icon that he in turn wipes on parts of his body, a magic ritual older than the Nazarene.

Outside Manila, the most colorful fiesta is that of Lucban, Quezon, in May, which celebrates the feast day of San Isidro de Labrador, patron saint of farmers. Called the *pahiyas*, this fiesta is a thanksgiving for a good harvest. People make colored rice wafers called *kiping,* which they hang outside their windows and doors together with fruits, vegetables, and grain.

Towns situated on rivers celebrate feast days with water parades. Icons mounted on water carriages are paraded on the river rather than on the streets. The devotees ride gaily decorated *banca* or immerse themselves in the water. In some areas, water throwing, reminiscent of a Thai practice, is allowed. The most famous of these water celebrations are found in the town of Gumaca in Quezon and in Naga in the Bicol region.

Opposite: **Quiapo's fervent devotees escort the Nazarene on his annual feast day in exchange for graces bestowed.**

Above: **Kiping clustered like giant translucent petals in various shades of pink, yellow, and green, and woven palm hats are hung outside a house as offerings (pahiyas) to honor San Isidro de Labrador, the patron saint of farmers.**

Opposite: **Ati-Atihan with the Santo Niño.** Christian and pagan elements come together during this riotous celebration lasting three days.

Below: ***Santacruzan*** participants.

FOLK RELIGIOUS FESTIVALS

Strong animist elements are felt in many religious festivals. The Ati-Atihan of Kalibo in Aklan Province, for example, is a local Mardi Gras held in honor of the Santo Niño ("SUN-to NIN-yoh"), the Christ Child. Revelers, their faces blackened with soot, go around town to the beat of drums and rhythmic shouts of *"Hala bira!"* The procession snakes frenzied along the narrow streets of Kalibo, pious women clutching Santo Niño icons to their bosoms rub elbows with hedonists drunk with the heart-pounding beat of the mountain tribes.

May is the month of Mary. Devotion to her takes the form of daily floral offerings by young girls. This culminates in the *Flores de Mayo,* a parade of the prettiest girls in all their finery walking beneath flower arches amidst candles and lights. In the cities, however, this has turned into a virtual fashion show, the girls' designer gowns more important than the devotion. Another version, the *Santacruzan,* reenacts Queen Helena's search for the Holy Cross. It is in essence a parade of biblical characters and allegorical figures. The major roles are still taken by the prettiest women.

Then there is the fisherman's festival called the *caracol,* a procession of pagoda-like boats used to carry venerated saints. Leafy branches are waved in their path by those who need miracles and blessings. These activities are accompanied by the music of a brass band and energetic water-splashing.

A Moslem girl dances to an Islamic dance celebration on Simunul Island in Tawi-Tawi Province.

OTHER FESTIVALS

Not to be outdone by their Filipino compatriots, the Chinese-Filipinos take out their firecrackers to celebrate the Lunar New Year, or the Spring Festival. In a land where there is no spring, they hand out *tikoy* (glutinous rice) to friends, prepare red packets of money for children, and engage lion dancers to visit their stores to ensure another year of good luck.

In southern Mindanao, Filipino Moslems observe the various Islamic festivals such as Hari Raya Puasa, the birth of Mohammed, and Ramadan.

The Shrine of Valor on top of Mount Samat in Bataan Province, central Luzon. A memorial to the war dead of World War II.

OFFICIAL HOLIDAYS

January 1	New Year's Day
April 9	Bataan Day
May 1	Labor Day
June 12	Independence Day
December 30	Rizal Day

January 1, a nonreligious holiday, is always considered part of Christmas. The New Year is greeted with firecrackers and fireworks at exactly 12 midnight, after which a lavish meal is shared. April 9 commemorates the bleakest time in Philippine history, when the combined American-Filipino forces were forced to surrender to the Japanese after a valiant last stand. June 12, 1898, was the first time the Filipinos declared their independence from a colonizer. This was made possible by the death of a great man, José Rizal, on December 30, 1896.

FOOD

FILIPINO FOOD depends mainly on what can be gathered from one's surroundings. The Philippines being a rice producing country, the staple food is rice. The long shoreline enables fishermen to cultivate the riches of the sea. Rice and fish therefore comprise the basic Filipino meal. Food is cooked simply and flavored by ingredients found in the vicinity. Fish or meat can be stewed with *kangkong* (leafy water vegetable), string beans or radishes, and soured tamarind or native lemon. As coconut is abundant, it is also a major ingredient in many Filipino dishes. Coconut milk is used with fish, meat, or vegetables. Its flesh can be mixed with other fruits for a salad or cooked with sugar and candied. Sugar is equally abundant, and the Filipino has developed an incorrigible sweet tooth. A meal is never complete without dessert, the more sinful the better. Compared with the spicy food of the rest of Southeast Asia, Filipino food can be considered bland. It may be seen as food for the more sensitive palate.

Opposite: **A stall in the market sells all types of agricultural produce from the farmlands of the Philippines.**

Left: **The Philippine seas yield a rich harvest of seafood, an important food staple.**

A MIXED TABLE

Filipino food is as mixed as Filipino ancestry. From the Spanish the natives got dishes with sauces such as *morcon* (beef with pork fat inserted inside it), *pochero* (beef, chicken, and pork chunks with cabbage, green beans, and the Spanish sausage *chorizo de Bilbao*), and that great culinary delight called *paella* (rice-seafood-meat dish). From the Chinese came different kinds of noodles that the Filipinos turned into *pancit bihon, pancit canton,* and the more Filipino *pancit palabok* and *pancit malabon.* Spring rolls and soy sauce are more savory borrowings from the kitchens of Cathay.

Filipino cuisine has evolved over the centuries from many foreign influences, including the Chinese. Modern Filipino households still relish Chinese *mi* or noodles.

American influence came mostly in terms of easy-to-prepare food. Hamburgers, for example, are now a fixture in Filipino life. Italian spaghetti has been sweetened to suit Filipino tastebuds and is considered party fare.

Most of the native concoctions come in the form of *kakanin*, a variety of rice cakes. However, there are also some dishes which are distinctly national. These are the *adobo* ("ADO-boh"), a dark stew of chicken and pork; the *dinuguan*, stew cooked in pig's blood; *bagoong*, a shrimp paste with an off-putting smell; and *balut*, boiled duck's egg with a half-formed chick. The latter two are formidable for those who have not acquired the taste, and eating them is considered the ultimate test of a foreigner's adjustment to Philippine life.

Halo-halo, meaning "mix-mix," is a typical dessert made with shaved ice, beans, gelatin, milk, and whatever else the maker can conjure into a tall sundae glass.

DELECTABLE TREATS

To satisfy their sweet tooth, Filipinos learned to concoct a variety of sweets and desserts. Among the more famous are:

bibingka—rice cakes made of glutinous rice.

suman—rice cakes wrapped in coconut or banana leaves.

yema—candies made of egg yolk and milk.

leche flan—egg custard.

ube—yam with milk.

ginatan—yam, sweet potato, and banana in coconut milk.

halo-halo—beans, sago, banana, yam, and gelatin in crushed ice and milk.

mais con hielo—sweet corn kernels in crushed ice and milk.

pastillas de leche—candied carabao's milk.

sorbetes—local ice cream.

Different kinds of fruit preserves and jams are stocked in kitchen cabinets in case there is a shortage of sweets.

Filipino culture revolves around rice. Besides being the main staple, rice features greatly in Filipino delicacies and every household has its *suman* wrapped in many different ways.

RICE

The first thing Filipino children learn in the kitchen is how to cook rice. They wash the grain, make sure the water reaches the second joint of their middle finger and set it over low a heat. They learn that they must turn off the heat at the right time, not too early, not too late, and that rice is allowed to cook in its own steam before it is served.

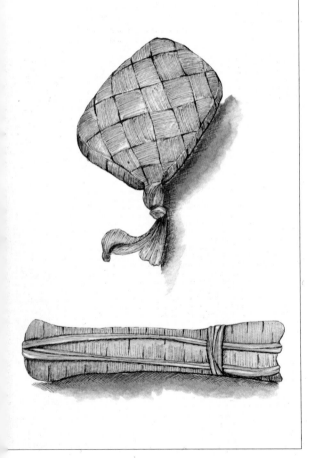

Rice, boiled or fried, is a meal staple, but on special occasions, special varieties like the *milagrosa* is served. Glutinous rice can be cooked into a hundred types of *kakanin* so dear to the Filipino's heart. During Christmas, the most popular rice sweet is *bibingka,* rice with coconut, egg, and milk baked in charcoal. Some people go for *puto bumbong,* glutinous rice combined with *pirurutong* that gives it a bluish tinge. Almost every province has its own *suman,* wrapped rice cakes. Some are wrapped in coconut fronds, some in banana leaf. The wrappers themselves are works of art and add to the enjoyment of the eating. Mixed with cocoa, rice becomes *champorado,* every child's favorite snack, usually eaten with something salty like dried fish. Ground, rice becomes *galapong,* an ingredient necessary to other rice-based dishes such as *puto* (steamed rice cakes), *pinaltok* (rice dough rolled into balls and immersed in sweet coconut milk), and *biko* (rice cooked in sugar). When eaten with grated coconut and aniseeds, it becomes *palitaw.* Rice gruel is generally fed to the sick, but when combined with chicken, it becomes *arroz caldo;* with tripe, it becomes *goto.*

THE EATING RITUAL

For the Filipino, food not only feeds the body but the soul as well. Eating is a ritual that allows one to touch base with family and friends. There is hardly an occasion when food is not served. A casual neighborly visit can result in a tray of spring rolls or a plate of noodles being served. Wakes, a basketball game, or a shopping jaunt are all oppurtunities to share food.

Most Filipinos eat with a fork and a spoon. Nevertheless, there are some things that can be relished only with the use of the hands. For the Filipino, this is fried rice and dried fish.

Filipinos always share their food. If your seatmate on a bus opens a package of chips, he or she will offer you some. House guests are always served food and drinks, and if they unexpectedly come in the middle of a meal, they will be asked to join in sampling the food. It would probably be discomfiting for the host if he had not cooked anything special on that day, so guests may decline the invitation to be polite. Repeated invitations, though, may mean that the host may be hurt if one does not eat anything, so it is wise to oblige him.

The Filipino's hospitality extends to the domain of food and guests are always served first.

113

WHERE TO EAT

Because the Filipino loves to eat, practically all kinds of restaurants can be found in Manila—French, Indian, Vietnamese—you name it, you'll find it. In the past, Filipinos ate out to try something they did not have at home. But now, with the introduction of posh native restaurants, local cooking has acquired glamor. Some native restaurants specialize in regional fare. The best, however, according to most food critics, is found

Below: **Small-time vendors, such as this man with his colorful ice-cream cart, offer a wide range of delicious local culinary fare.**

not in plush eateries, but in roadside ones patronized by laborers and jeepney drivers. Here, customers peek into glass compartments or pots and point out the dishes they prefer, thus the name *turo-turo* (point-point). During a coffee break, one can have hot noodles or porridge very cheaply from the cart hawker. Local ice cream is sold from ornately-designed carts. Cola comes in bottles but if you do not want to pay a deposit, the drink will be poured into a plastic bag and a straw inserted.

Native restaurants are quite popular with tourists because of their exotic ambience. Some plush restaurants encourage customers to eat with their hands the traditional way. Wooden or wicker plates lined with banana leaves add to the novelty. Coconut juice is served still inside the coconut.

A more earthy version can be found in the market areas, but competition is so stiff stalls have to employ criers who will cajole or even force customers to patronize their stalls. A newcomer caught between two fierce criers can be the object of tugging and pulling.

ADOBO WITH CHICKEN

2 ¼lb	roasting chicken
1 tsp	salt
1 tsp	ground black pepper
½ tsp	ground paprika
12	finely chopped cloves of garlic
2	bay leaves
⅔ cup	spiced vinegar, lemon or lime juice
⅔ cup	water
3 tsp	oil
¾	skinned, quartered tomatoes
2	sprigs of corriander leaves to garnish

1. Mix salt, pepper, and paprika.
2. Rotate dry chicken pieces in above mixture.
3. Place chicken in pan with bay leaves and sprinklings of garlic.
4. Add mixture of lemon juice and water to chicken and slowly bring to a boil, then simmer, rotating chicken till tender and liquid has been reduced to 5 tbsp.
5. Remove chicken from liquid in pan, drain and dry it.
6. Heat oil in another pan on high heat and quickly fry chicken pieces till golden brown.
7. Serve with remaining cooking liquid on top, garnished with tomato quarters and corriander, accompanied by rice and a bowl of soya sauce.

NO TIME TO EAT

Most Filipinos take eating seriously and take time to savor their meals. The pace of life, however, has become faster and quick meals are in demand. The last decade saw the mushrooming of fast food centers. No shopping mall is ever without one. The wide variety gives one innumerable choices that can be had in a jiffy. American chains such as McDonald's, Pizza Hut, Wendy's, Shakey's, and the Philippines' most successful chain, Jollibee, are a busy person's recourse. People need not step out of their homes or offices anymore because these stores deliver. It is also not strange to see elderly women carrying heavy baskets into elevators of plush offices. They are carrying plastic bags with lunches previously ordered or to be sold to employees who have no time to line up in the canteens. These women are not supposed to be allowed entry, but the free lunch they give the guards allows them free passage.

FOOD FOR THE GODS

The fiesta is not only a social and religious celebration, it is also a culinary occasion. No self-respecting host would put everyday dishes on a fiesta table if he can help it. The dish may be as homey as *dinuguan* or *sinigang* (sour soup), but there is always an added extra to make it special.

If there is one word that describes fiesta food, it is "rich." Pork leg *estofado* is simmered in burned sugar sauce, and thickened with the nectar of ripe banana. *Embotido* is meat roll stuffed with egg, olives, and relish mixed with ground meat and steamed to perfection. *Galantina* is shredded or diced chicken flavored with broth, milk, and spices.

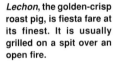

Lechon, the golden-crisp roast pig, is fiesta fare at its finest. It is usually grilled on a spit over an open fire.

Lumpiang ubod (coconut spring roll) is only the softest pith of the coconut sautéed with shrimp and pork, wrapped in thin egg wrappers, and sometimes topped by a gravy seasoned with ground garlic. There is *lapu-lapu,* a large fish steamed and garnished with mayonnaise, relish, peas, corn, parsley, and shredded carrots. As for the centerpiece, a four-month-old roasted pig called *lechon* is displayed in all its crisp glory, tempting eaters to bite into its red crunchy skin. It is accompanied by a thick liver sauce.

The desserts can only be described as sinful—a curse to the dieter, a delight to the gourmet. Egg custard is made with duck's eggs for a creamier effect and doused with burned sugar sauce. Gelatins in all colors contain suspended fruits and raisins in mid-jello and are topped with whipped cream or milk. Strips of coconut, all soft and fluffy, and cooked with aromatic *pandan* leaves, make up the *macapuno.*

An eclectic Manila cuisine of local *paella* rice, Chinese spring roll, raw fish vinaigrette, crabs in coco-milk, and fancy fruit juices.

FRUITS

Philippine fruits are mostly tropical. The most common are bananas (different varieties), papaya, watermelon, rockmelon, avocado, soursop, jackfruit, mango, pineapple, guava, and native orange. Seasonal fruits include lanzon, rambutan, and *siniguela* (green berry). Some fruits can be found only in the north or the south. Strawberries can be grown only in the cool highlands of the Mountain provinces, while mangosteens and durians can be found only in Mindanao.

Fruits are eaten mostly as dessert or snacks, but they also have medicinal and superstitious value. Papaya, for example, is a cure for constipation, while bananas provide good roughage. Green mangoes are craved by expectant mothers; guavas can cause appendicitis. *Siniguela* can cause diarrhea, while the black *duhat* (cherry) should not be eaten by expectant mothers lest their children develop a dark complexion.

KITCHEN UTENSILS

In the old days, kitchenware meant an earthen pot, a bamboo dipper, and possibly the iron wok that the Chinese introduced to the Philippines. It is believed that rice can only be properly cooked in an earthen pot because the pores of the clay preserve the flavor. The *sandok* ("SUN-dok"), made of half a coconut shell tied to a stick, is the native ladle. The *kawali* ("kah-WALL-ih"), native wok, does the frying. Its bigger sister, the *kawa,* is used mostly during fiestas when people by the hundreds have to be fed. Food preparation is done on a bamboo table or a *paminggalan* where plates and glasses are left to dry. A heavy stone grinder is used to create the sweets and rice cakes Filipinos are fond of. Water is stored in a clay jar with a big body and a small opening. Old folks swear that water from the jar is definitely sweeter and fresher than water from the tap.

The fast pace of modern life cannot afford the patient waiting done by the cooks of old. Today, slow fire means a setting on the microwave. Grandmothers would turn in their graves if they knew that their grandchildren were eating rice cooked in the microwave.

Above: **Molds in the shapes of fish, birds, and other designs that reflect the local environment are used for making delectable pastry and sweets.**

Left: **The** *kawali,* **or Chinese wok, and the** *sandok* **are still used extensively in Filipino kitchens despite the introduction of modern appliances.**

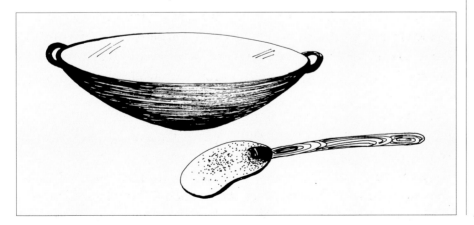

119

Below: **Tuba** from coconut trees are collected in bamboo containers which are fastened to the trees. After gathering a tree's sap, the gatherer crosses to the next tree by way of bamboo poles connecting them.

Opposite: **A tagayan** drinking session.

OF FILIPINOS AND SPIRITS

When Magellan set out to fight that upstart of a chieftain called Lapu-Lapu, he and his men had just been to a feast where they were given a sweetish liquid that puts one in high spirits. Strangely, before the day was over, Magellan and his men were defeated. The sweetish liquid is called *tuba*, a kind of coconut wine made from the sap of an unopened coconut bud. The tip of the bud is lopped off and the sap is allowed to flow for the whole day. Tree bark is mixed with the liquid to give it a reddish hue.

During the American period, some ingenious drinker made *lambanog*, a powerful, clear distilled liquid that burns as it goes down. It is made from coconut fermented with chewing gum or apples in a bottle for a month. These two alcoholic drinks are popular in coconut-producing provinces such as Laguna, Batangas, and Quezon.

Up north, the Ilocanos have discovered that sugarcane makes good wine. They ferment sugarcane juice in huge jars that are buried under their houses. The result is a wine called *basi*. The Ifugaos discovered that applying the *tuba* process to rice or corn can produce another version of the wine. Not to be outdone by the West, it did not take Filipinos long to concoct their own beer, the San Miguel brand, internationally acknowledged as one of the best.

To the fun-loving Filipino, there is always a reason for drinking. On street corners, men drink from one glass which is passed around in the spirit of camaraderie. One shot is called a *tagay* ("TAH-gai"). Refusing a *tagay* means loss of face to the one who offered and this may lead to a brawl. In the countryside, women may toss back a glassful without batting an eyelid and may even shame the men by outdrinking them.

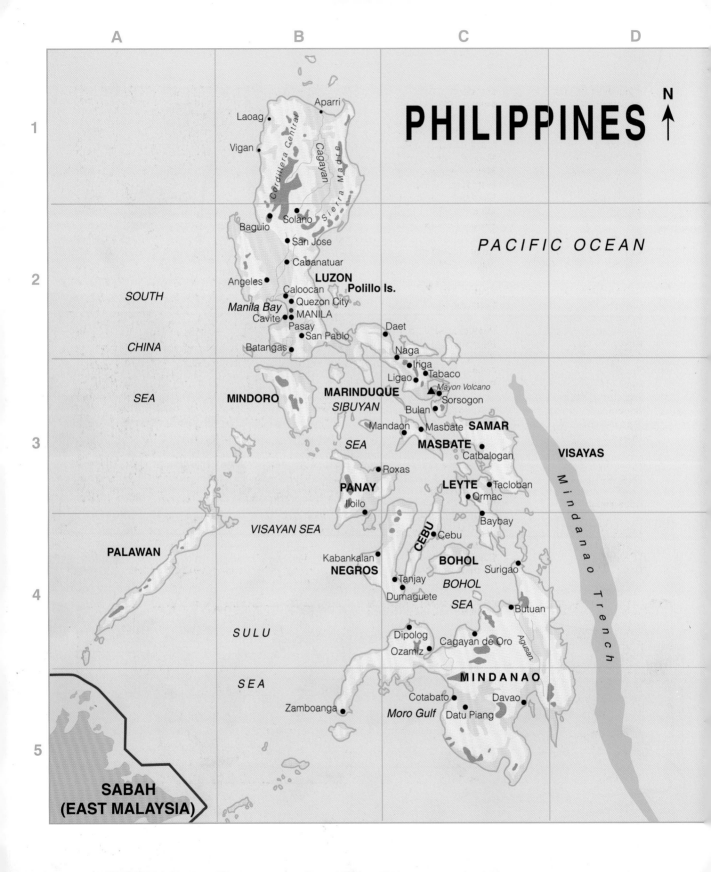

PHILIPPINES N↑

A   **B**   **C**   **D**

1

Aparri
Laoag
Vigan

Cordillera Central
Cagayan
Sierra Madre

PACIFIC OCEAN

Solano
Baguio
San Jose
Cabanatuar
Angeles
LUZON
Caloocan
Polillo Is.
Quezon City
Manila Bay
Cavite
MANILA
Pasay
San Pablo
Batangas

Daet

SOUTH

Naga
Iriga
Ligao
Tabaco
▲ *Mayon Volcano*
Sorsogon
Bulan

CHINA

2

MARINDUQUE
SIBUYAN
MINDORO

Mandaon
Masbate
SAMAR

SEA

SEA
MASBATE
Catbalogan
VISAYAS

3

Roxas

PANAY
Iloilo

LEYTE
Tacloban
Ormac

Mindanao Trench

VISAYAN SEA

CEBU
Cebu
Baybay

PALAWAN

Kabankalan
BOHOL
Surigao

NEGROS
Tanjay
BOHOL

SULU
Dumaguete
SEA
Butuan

Dipolog
Cagayan de Oro
Agusan
Ozamiz

4

SEA

MINDANAO

Zamboanga
Cotabato
Davao

Moro Gulf
Datu Piang

5

**SABAH
(EAST MALAYSIA)**

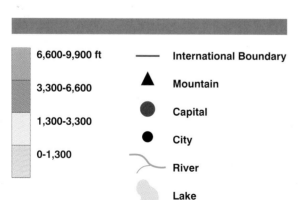

6,600-9,900 ft	——	International Boundary
3,300-6,600	▲	Mountain
1,300-3,300	●	Capital
0-1,300	●	City
	～	River
	⬮	Lake

QUICK NOTES

LAND AREA
115,830 square miles

POPULATION
65.8 million

CAPITAL
Manila

NUMBER OF ISLANDS
7,107

MAJOR ISLANDS
Luzon, Mindanao, the Visayas

HIGHEST POINT
Mount Apo (9,692 feet)

OFFICIAL LANGUAGES
Filipino, based on Tagalog, and English

MAJOR RELIGIONS
Christianity (83% Roman Catholicism, 9% Protestant), Islam, Buddhism, Taoism

CURRENCY
Peso ($1 = 25 pesos)

MAIN EXPORTS
Sugar cane, coconut, pineapple, garments, manpower, electronic equipment.

FLAG
The flag consists of a white triangle on the extreme left and two horizontal strips of blue and red. In times of war, the red strip is placed on top. The triangle has a yellow sun with eight rays, representing the eight provinces that revolted against Spanish rule. The three stars at the triangle's corners symbolize the three major groups of islands: Luzon, the Visayas, and Mindanao.

IMPORTANT ANNIVERSARIES
April 9—Fall of Bataan (1942)
June 12—Independence Day (1898)
December 30—Rizal Day

LEADERS IN POLITICS
Emilio Aguinaldo—First president of the Philippine Republic, who declared independence on June 12, 1898.
Manuel Quezon—First president of the Commonwealth (1935–42).
Ferdinand Marcos—Ruled the Philippines for 20 years; toppled by the People Power revolution in 1986.
Corazon Aquino—Swept to power by the People Power revolution in 1986; decided not to run for reelection in 1992.
Fidel Ramos—Won presidency in election on May 11, 1992.

GLOSSARY

amor propio ("ah-MOR PRO-pio") Self-esteem, similar to the concept of face.

asuang ("AH-swung") A creature of the underworld.

babaylan ("BY-BY-lun") Faith healer. Shaman.

barangay ("bar-RUNG-gai") A pre-Spanish Filipino community. The most basic political unit.

barong ("BAH-rong") Men's traditional wear.

barrio ("BAH-rio") Village.

compadrazgo ("COM-pud-DRAS-coh") Non-blood kinship ties usually established during baptisms, weddings, or any kind of sponsorship.

delicadeza Social propriety.

galleons Spanish ships that sailed between Manila and Acapulco laden with goods for Spain.

hiya ("HIH-yah") Shame.

Indios Spanish derogatory term for the natives.

karaoke A singing performance with the aid of a microphone and music videos. It can also be a club providing the neccessary set-up.

kristo ("KRIS-toh") Ringmaster at a cockfighting match.

mestizos ("mis-TEE-sohs") Of mixed parentage.

pakikisama ("pa-KI-ki-SUM-muh") The art of maintaining smooth interpersonal relationships.

pamanhikan ("PAH-man-HE-khan") The formal asking of a woman's hand in marriage.

Pinoy The Filipinos' nickname for themselves.

BIBLIOGRAPHY

Bjener, Tamiko, *Children of the World: Philippines,* Gareth Stevens, Milwaukee, WI, 1987.

Fernando, Gilda, *We Live in the Philippines,* Franklin Watts, New York, 1986.

Fuentes, Vilma, *Pearl Makers: Six Stories about the Children in the Philippines,* Friendship Press, New York, 1989.

Haskins, James, *Corazon Aquino: Leader of the Philippines,* Enslow Publications, Hillside, NJ, 1988.

Sonneborn, Liz, *The Philippines,* Chelsea House, New York, 1988.

INDEX

INDEX

INDEX